Yacht Navigation—My Way

by the same author
THE SHELL PILOT TO THE ENGLISH CHANNEL
1. Harbours on the South Coast of England
Ramsgate to the Scillies
THE SHELL PILOT TO THE ENGLISH CHANNEL
2. Harbours in Northern France and the Channel Islands
Dunkerque to Brest
THE SHELL GUIDE TO YACHT NAVIGATION (BRITISH EDITION)

Yacht Navigation—My Way

Captain J. O. Coote, Royal Navy

W. W. Norton & Company

NEW YORK  LONDON

First published in 1987
by Faber and Faber Limited
3 Queen Square London WC1N 3AU

It is regretted that neither the book's sponsor, nor its author,
nor the publisher can accept responsibility for errors or
omissions, especially those brought about by changes made
by harbor and navigation authorities after the time of
going to press.

Library of Congress Cataloging-in-Publication Data
Coote, J. O. (John O.)
Yacht navigation—my way.
(A Shell guide)
Includes index.
1. Navigation.   2. Yachts and yachting.   I. Title.
VK555.C85 1988   623.89′0247971   88-3917

ISBN 0-393-03326-0

W. W. Norton & Company, Inc., 500 Fifth Avenue, New York, N. Y. 10110
W. W. Norton & Company Ltd., 37 Great Russell Street, London WC1B 3NU
1   2   3   4   5   6   7   8   9   0

For
CONGO
who does it his way—
microchips with everything.

CONTENTS

FOREWORD
by Robin Knox-Johnston, C.B.E.

Navigation sounds so simple—just the art of finding your destination from your departure point. It does not matter whether you are going halfway round the world, or just popping along the coast to the next port, you are still going to navigate your way. The differences may seem immense: the one seeing no land for months on end and finding his way by the sun, stars or Sat-Nav; and the other probably doing it all by eye, but both are performing the same function.

The professional navigator learns all sorts of tricks to help him to find his position, and he also learns shortcuts to make the job easier. However, he still needs to master the basics, without relying on all the modern aids that have made navigation today so simple. Before the days of Decca, I was a young watchkeeper in a small passenger ship in the Persian Gulf when we ran into a thickish, low-lying sandstorm. Visibility was reduced to a couple of miles, with the horizon obscured from the bridge, when the radar packed up and we were left to find our way by dead reckoning. The captain decided, however, that he wanted a check. So he had the gangway lowered down to sea level, and I was sent down with a sextant to get a sight. The trick was to get a clear horizon by reducing the height of eye so that a sight was possible. We got a position line, made Kuwait in safety, and I had learned another useful lesson.

Modern yacht navigation is increasingly dependent on electronic aids, which are excellent and very accurate. However, many yachtsmen have not had the time, nor the experience, to learn what to do when the power fails or the fuse blows and these magic aids cease to function. The result can be worry at best, fear at worst, and probably a crew who will be a lot less keen to come sailing again. It is not enough to know how to work the most complicated of modern navigational aids. It is as important to know the basics behind how to navigate, so that, whatever the situation, you have a good idea of where you are and where you should be heading.

These sorts of skills can only be learned from a really experienced navigator, preferably someone who has received a thorough training in the fundamentals, made mistakes over the years and profited from them, and has the ability to pass the knowledge on in an easy-to-understand and amusing manner—as Johnnie Coote demonstrates in this book.

I have always had the greatest respect for those who can navigate completely blind, as a submariner has to beneath the sea, and he learned his trade in submarines. The concentration and sheer professionalism leave their mark. Certainly, years later in 1971, when we sailed together with Sir Max Aitken in *Crusade*, Johnnie was a very wily and accurate navigator. He was also great fun to sail with, and that, fundamentally, is what navigation and sailing should be all about.

I address this book to the weekend sailor who wants to graduate from his one-design dinghy or Boston whaler in an estuary and go farther afield. It is intended to lift the veil of mystique which surrounds the navigator's art and show that making a coastal or even offshore passage without undue worry or delay is simpler than most cross-country trips on secondary roads in the family jalopy.

If he feels like indulging himself in electronic push-button aids to navigation, this book sounds a note of caution on the degree of accuracy and infallibility claimed for most of them.

There are many admirable textbooks on the subject, some of them dwelling at greater length than I do on the theory behind the practice. For example, I make no attempt to encourage taking star sights from a yacht, not due to their slightly greater complexity but because the average conditions from the deck of a yacht at twilight are most likely to yield misleading results, even for comparatively experienced navigators.

My approach is to instruct by recalling my own experience of navigating cruising and racing boats in many waters for nearly half a century. There are few mistakes I have not made in my time. It may surprise some that many of the lessons I have learned were drawn from years of blind, three-dimensional navigation in submarines.

The book is enriched by Graham Parrish's meticulous illustrations and by Major-General Jim Gavin's constructive criticism after running his practiced eye over my manuscript. Sappers make great navigators, whether finding their way around mine fields or up Mount Everest—he has done both.

John Coote
May 1987

This is a new book written by an experienced navigator who prefers to rely on his own observations, first principles and the instruments he considers to be the Bare Necessities: a compass and a chart on which to plot the data provided by a log and depth sounder.

Anything beyond that is a luxury which undoubtedly simplifies the navigator's task when it all functions correctly. But once in a while even the most sophisticated (and expensive) electronic aids falter. Or he may be dangerously misled by a sight taken with an ill-defined horizon or a radio bearing under adverse conditions. The navigator should always assume the worst case until it is proved otherwise. The real skill comes down to knowing what degree of reliability is to be placed on all the inputs, without bothering too much about theory.

This book cuts out the mystique and is a refreshing new approach, readily comprehensible to first-time navigators.

All this is illustrated by line drawings of exceptional clarity by Graham Parrish and punctuated by the author's own reminiscences of over forty years' cruising and racing all over the world, including fourteen Fastnets, eight Bermuda Races, the Sydney-Hobart, and winning the Southern Ocean Racing Conference series off Florida, to say nothing (much) of Antigua Sail Week and two transatlantic crossings, one of them under jury rig.

While on liaison duty with the U.S. Submarine Force in the late fifties the author was a member of COMSUBLANT's hatchet squad which selected the winning submarine for the Force "E." His task was to evaluate their navigation and combat plotting performance. Later he became the first non-American to make an extended patrol in a nuclear submarine, aboard the U.S.S. *Nautilus* on her first visit to Europe when she took part in Operation Rum Tub.

He is Commodore of the most exclusive of all yacht clubs, the L.Y.S. (Let's-sail-now Yacht Squadron), membership in which is confined to those who have set sail after midnight in Force 7 wearing dinner jackets.

1 THE BARE NECESSITIES

Some half-baked people with half-decked dinghies make impressive coastal passages without any aids to navigation beyond a road map. Ironically they often get away with it. But sooner or later others will have to go out of their way and even risk their necks to get them out of difficulties of their own making.

I am indebted to Captain Ian McKay, the harbormaster at Chichester, England, for the tale of a young couple who sought to oblige a friend by delivering his newly acquired 21-ft dayboat from the Hamble to its new home at Lechlade on the upper reaches of the Thames via the Straits of Dover—a little matter of 300 miles. The voyage ended on the Looe Rocks off Selsey, just 40 miles along the route. When the lifeboat took them off in a rising gale they clutched their sole aid to navigation for the voyage—a road map of England. The battered remains of the boat were then lashed onto a borrowed trailer and delivered to the owner via Winchester and Newbury in under four hours.

Nowhere in England or in North America is there any statutory inhibition to stop would-be Francis Chichesters from putting down a deposit at the boat show and setting sail in a cloud of euphoria. This especially applies to first-time power-boat owners with only a checkbook or a ferry timetable for a navigation manual.

The easiest way to learn is alongside a practical navigator who has already made most of the classic mistakes and not a few original ones in his time—a fully paid-up member of the Reciprocal Club, or one who failed to note that the chart's depths were in feet and not meters, misidentified a watery light by failing to check its characteristics by stopwatch, or cutting a corner in overfamiliar waters on a falling tide without a glance at the chart. As I have done.

He or she will soon teach you that the whole art lies in always assuming the worst case until it is proved otherwise. This proposition underlies my efforts to make yacht navigation a matter of commonsense filtering of observed data.

There are other ways to learn. For example some local authorities and many yacht clubs run winter evening classes based on the syllabus approved by the U.S. Coast Guard up to various levels of competence as yacht navigators. You can even get audio or videocassettes to augment the impressive list of textbooks on the subject. For details check the classified advertisements in the yachting magazines.

As for our friends who ended up on the rocks off Selsey, I'll send them a copy of this book in the slight hope that they have not lost their taste for seagoing altogether.

For the owner of the average family cruiser who wants to explore not-too-distant horizons there are certain Bare Necessities beyond the inventory of safety equipment needed for sailing in any weather (navigation lights, radar reflector, foghorn, safety harnesses and lifejackets). They are:

1. A compass
2. Charts and the means of using them
3. A means of measuring how much water is under the keel
4. A method of measuring distance run and/or speed.

The compass

An accurate compass that can be easily read by the helmsman under all circumstances is essential. It is not an item to economize on. It may end up costing $300, but it will last a lifetime. Installing it in the optimum position should take priority over all other considerations.

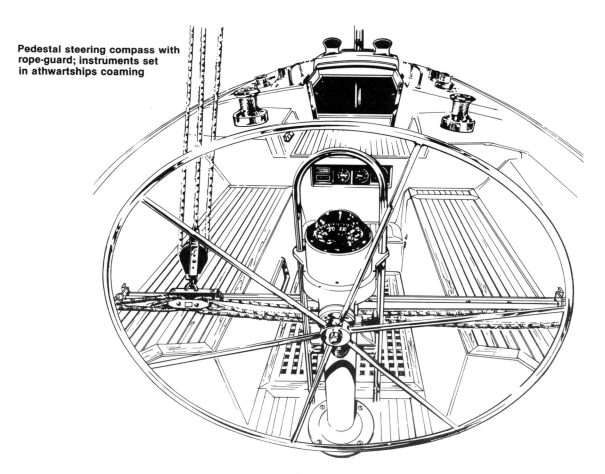

Pedestal steering compass with rope-guard; instruments set in athwartships coaming

In a yacht with *wheel steering* the most satisfactory location is on a pedestal in the center line immediately before the wheel. Ideally the compass should:

(a) Have a gimballed compass card inside an oil-filled magnified glass bowl with optimum damping against the boat's movement in a sea way. It should be gimballed without interference up to 45° of heel.

(b) Read 0—360° using 1- or 2-figure white numbers in 20° steps. I like to see the cardinal points shown as letters (N, E, S and W), with unnumbered intermediate headings every 5°, but otherwise the card must be simple and easy to read from wherever the helmsman chooses to steer. It is useful if there are gimballed vertical lubber's lines marking the abeam bearings as well as those lined up fore-and-aft. Sitting the boat out to weather, it is easy to sail on a "minus-90°" course; e.g., while sailing a course of 340°, sit out to starboard and sail the boat on 250° using the port-beam lubber's line. They also permit a crew member to watch the ship's head if the helmsman is concentrating on other instruments.

(c) Have independent illumination of the compass card controlled by an on-off switch and a separate dimmer rheostat located down below under cover. It is undesirable to have the compass illumination on the same switch as the navigation lights.

(d) A detachable nonmagnetic binnacle cover is necessary to protect the main compass from damage in harbor. As a rule these fold over to expose the helmsman's side of the compass card, but it is best to stow it below at sea. There is no point in distracting the helmsman by asking for the heading when someone can read off the reciprocal and add 180°.

(e) The means of adjusting the compass (magnets) should be protected against accidental physical interference but easily accessible to the adjuster.

For yachts with *tiller steering* there are several options,

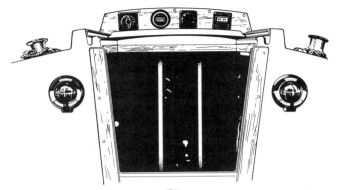

For a boat with tiller steering — two compasses set in for'ard cockpit bulkhead with instruments overhead

depending on the size of the cockpit and the likelihood of having other crew members blocking the helmsman's view of the compass. The criteria outlined above for the pedestal-mounted compass apply wherever practicable.

(f) A bracket-mounted compass being a vertical surface with external gimballing is prone to being snagged by sheets or lurching crew. It can be unshipped and stowed below in harbor, always bearing in mind the risk of upsetting the ship's magnetic error in the compass (deviation).

(g) Shelf-mounted compasses, flush-fitting with the deck or thwart, tend to be sited close to the main magnetic interference (engine, electric cables, magnetic influences in other instruments). On a beamy boat it may be worth having two shelf-mounted compasses, one mounted on deck each side immediately before the helmsman's upwind steering position. The trouble begins when they disagree with one another.

(h) If the hatchway is in the center-line, bulkhead-mounted compasses are off center. The effect of this is psychological rather than practical. There are also problems lurking the other side of the bulkhead if there are other nav-aids or cables close by. But many such compasses have the bonus of a clinometer measuring the angle of heel under them. This is a much neglected aid to making a boat go faster, if its design is such that it needs to be sailed as nearly upright as possible.

(i) The standard compass can be mounted in the coachroof, subject to the helmsman's clear view of it in all conditions.

(j) A recent development is to depend on remote-reading displays transmitted from a master compass. There are also those that include the compass readout in a single display console showing the whole range of nav-aids, from the log to wind data to the log and engine data (SIMRAD S-100 is one such). Some have even abandoned the use of the word compass by calling it the "Heading Reference Unit." Once you accustom yourself to a digital display of the ship's heading it has some advantages: for a start, the numbers are big enough to read, even by a helmsman with spray-drenched spectacles. Once the master compass has been tucked away far from all local interference it has a high degree of built-in stability. There is no reason why it should lose anything in transmitting to a slave display unit. A large-scale digital readout mounted on the mast under the boom gooseneck is now in fashion.

Compasses for *powerboats* need not cater for more than 15° angle of heel but should have shockproof mounting and be sufficiently damped to keep a steady ship's head. Many have an external 0—360° ring which can be slewed round to get the desired course on to the lubber line. The helmsman then has to keep to the ordered course by aligning the compass card to the external ring.

Generally the steering compass in a powerboat is well away from the main source of the ship's magnetic interference—the engine. It is desirable to have it mounted so that it lies on or near the helmsman's line-of-sight while looking ahead. The quality of lookout which a helmsman can maintain within a sheltered wheelhouse is in any event greatly inferior to that from an open position, so the less distraction he has the better. That is why I prefer a compass suspended from overhead (see p. 29).

Secondary Compass

Although modern steering compasses are reliable and surprisingly accurate within their known limits of error (see p. 6) it is essential to have a spare primary compass on board. In a small boat a *hand-bearing compass* can serve this purpose.

These come in many shapes and sizes, dating back to the cumbersome ex-Service, teak-handled bowl variety with optical bearing prism. The handle's size was determined by the batteries needed to provide illumination, but nowadays most have built-in fluorescent lighting. These need a secure, dry stowage of their own, so are not as readily available on deck as they should be when the need arises. They weigh 3 lb each.

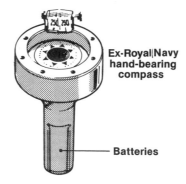

Ex-Royal Navy hand-bearing compass

Batteries

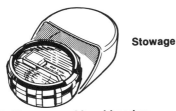

Stowage

Rubber covered hand-bearing compass with beta light

By far the best type is the 3-in-diameter mini-compass held in a 1-in-deep rubber collar. In the United States it is referred to as the "hockey puck." A tritium gas capsule (or beta light) provides excellent lighting. The human hand is as good as most gyrostabilized gimbals, so excellent bearings can be obtained, provided always that you give the mini-compass time to settle down after being yanked out of your oilskin pocket or wherever else it is stowed. In a jump of sea, when the compass card swings over and above the helmsman chasing the lubber line, it is essential to wait for a mean reading at either end of the swing.

Hand-bearing compasses have eliminated the need for azimuth rings or any other means of taking bearings directly from the steering compass by standing abaft the helmsman and observing the compass heading off the ship's fore-and-aft line.

A fair calibrating point for the latter is to put a bit of boat tape on the after end of the superstructure in transit with the base of the mast, having first verified it from the lubber line on the steering compass.

The hand-bearing compass is essential for watching the bearing of a converging ship or of progress against the tide on a passing headland—or a competing boat in a race. It is also the best way of checking the steering compass on an ocean passage using the azimuth of the sun when it is very low on the horizon (see p. 7). There are binoculars on sale with a bearing compass built-in, but their field of view is restricted, especially in a jump of sea.

Except in an emergency it is not practical to use the hand-bearing compass as a substitute steering compass. A small bracket-mounted compass (only 5 in diameter) in the vicinity of the chart table not only gives the navigator an on-the-spot check on the course being steered, but can be pressed into service as an alternate steering compass (see p. 34). This does not rate as one of the Bare Necessities, but at around $65 costs little more than the hand-bearing compass.

Finally if you have a radio D/F set it will have a small compass as part of the hand-held antenna, but I would not rate this as better than ±10° accuracy, no matter what the makers claim.

Installation
Most stock boats are sold with the compass already installed as the only standard nav-aid. The rest, from echo sounder to wind indicators, are customer options. Even so it is as well to check that the compass is fitted to the requirements listed above and is not affected by the motor or any electronic devices running. It is a fundamental requirement that the lubber line is set fore and aft. This is a matter best left to a boat yard.

Compass Errors
There are two variable sources of compass error which distinguish a magnetic compass from a gyro-compass reading degrees True. That is, on the normal mercator's-projection charts which we use, True North (360°T) is the vertical axis of the chart, up and down the page.

But magnetic compasses seek the North magnetic pole, which is a slowly meandering point located in the Arctic wastes nor'west of Greenland. This is 360°M. The first correction to be applied between the two is known as *Variation*. It is shown on the compass rose of all government charts as a separate pointer towards North (magnetic) which slews all the other 360° magnetic headings with it.

Thus a current chart of Nantucket Sound will show the variation to be around 15°45'W. Alongside the legend on the compass rose is the year on which this was correct, with a small annual correction to allow for the magnetic North Pole's meandering around. Unless you are using a very old chart, the difference is minimal and can be ignored. Often there are two or more magnetic compass roses on a chart; be sure to use the one nearest your position.

The other correction is to take account of the errors induced by local magnetic fields in the boat and its equipment. This is known as *Deviation* and has to be added or subtracted to the Variation.

Think True

Make a determined effort to get into the habit of navigating at all times in degrees True, because those are the lines you are going to draw on the chart. Furthermore all the information given on most charts or other navigation publications is in degrees True.

There are various mental aids to translate magnetic to True, of which the best known is:

Variation West—Compass best (higher number of degrees)
Variation East—Compass least (lower number of degrees)

This means simply that 10°W Variation will have the effect of the ship's magnetic compass reading 10° higher than True. Thus 250°M is the same as 240°T. If in doubt, as one sometimes is when tired or sailing in unaccustomed parts of the world, line up your parallel ruler on the compass rose to read 250°M and you will see on the outer ring that it is 240°T.

Exactly the same applies with Deviation. The slight complication is that a Deviation with a contrary name to the Variation has to be applied accordingly:

Variation 10°W   Deviation 3°W means that 240°T is the same as 253°M. Whereas
Variation 10°W   Deviation 3°E   results in 240°T being 247°M.

Always remember that while the navigation and general picture is being conducted in degrees True, the helmsman and any information from bearings observed will be in degrees magnetic. Don't attempt to confuse that issue, until the day when we have gyrocompasses in yachts. The helmsman's ordered course must be always magnetic.

Compass Corrections and Adjustment

On first installation the steering compass should be checked and adjusted professionally. Any marina office will produce an expert who will take the boat out with you and do this. First there will be a 360° swing through the cardinal points to identify the compass error on each 45° heading (Deviation). By moving magnets close to the compass card, these errors can be reduced or eliminated.

At the end of the day you will be presented with a Deviation Card and Certificate of Correction which should reduce Deviation to less than 3° on any heading. Usually it comes down to a figure so small that it can be ignored, except on long passages. The errors shown on the card should be symmetrical about Nil error (i.e., maximum W'ly Deviation should be nearly, but not exactly matched by the highest E'ly Deviation).

To steer a given magnetic course, the actual compass course to be steered is shown in the right column.

Don't forget this applies only to the steering compass, so

Deviation Card

STEERING COMPASS

Yacht: *Lulubelle XIII*
Date: 13 May 1987

Magnetic Course	Deviation	Compass Course
000°	1°E	359°
015°	1°E	014°
030°	2°E	028°
045°	3°E	042°
060°	3°E	057°
075°	2°E	073°
090°	1°E	089°
105°	1°E	104°
130°	0	130°
145°	0	145°
165°	1°W	166°
180°	1°W	181°
↓		
360°		

Signed: J. M. Fingers

be professionally checked and adjusted. The fact is that it need not be done unless it is seen to be necessary as the result of your own *ad hoc* checks. These are most important and should be carried out whenever the boat has been laid up ashore or left lying alongside on a constant heading for any length of time. It is dead simple. Take any distant transit of charted conspicuous points ashore and read off the compass heading when it is lined up ahead. Repeat the process with the transit dead astern. But if time does not permit, at least take a reading going along well-marked channels, where the true course can be taken off the chart.

On an ocean passage the best check on your compass is to take an azimuth (bearing) of any celestial body, but preferably the sun at low altitude. This is especially necessary in a steel boat. The easiest way is to take the sun's bearing when its lower limb is within half its diameter of the observed horizon. First you should know your latitude and declination to within 1°. Then simply enter the tables in the almanac which give "Sun's True Bearing at Rising and Setting." You can work it out ahead of time.

Thus for latitude 51°N and declination 10°N the sun's bearing on rising will be 074°True (N74°E). If the declination is 10°S then the True bearing would be 74° anticlockwise from due south or S74°E (i.e., 180° − 74° = 106°True).

Apply Variation to determine the compass error. The Deviation will only be correct for the ship's heading at the time of observation.

The easiest way is to point the boat directly at or away from the sun at the moment. Or use a hand-bearing compass.

Modern yacht compasses are reliable and surprisingly accurate, so don't worry unduly that they may suddenly let you down. Just watch out for the introduction of a new source of magnetic interference. I know of a steering compass which was mysteriously thrown off when a jerrican was moved from one

others, like the hand-bearing compass, do not have this fine tuning. Nor do they need it, since the accuracy of bearings read from them is usually well outside the swing of Deviations; in any case it will vary with the proximity of major ship's sources of magnetic interference on each occasion of taking a bearing.

There is much advice on how frequently the compass should

end of the cockpit locker to the other.

Once there was a cadet at Dartmouth who was so unhappy that he decided to "borrow" a 45-ft Admiralty launch and head for Spain. He did all his chartwork before creeping away during the middle watch, setting a course from Start Point to Ushant. Dawn found him off Alderney, where he was apprehended. He had no reason to believe that the compass had not been swung or adjusted for years. Yet when the police boarded him he declined a cigarette because smoking was forbidden at the College. His log showed that he had carefully switched off the motor for five minutes each hour, as he had been taught.

Charts

No matter what size or type of boat you sail in, if you intend taking it outside your local harbor limits a suitable inventory of up-to-date charts is essential.

It used to be the practice of chart agents to date-stamp each chart on the day you bought it. I make a point of noting it alongside the title in pencil. Next look to see when the chart was printed and the number of the latest small correction made as a result of a Notice to Mariners. On government charts all this information is on the bottom of the chart.

Imray charts give the date of printing inside the first cover and have a resumé of recent corrections on a fly sheet.

In 1950 I joined *Fandango* for the Santander Race returning via a race to Belle Île and cruising home. The owner was Gerald Potter, an unforgettable hairshirt Grenadier-turned-fisherman. I looked over the charts and found that they had all been bought from J. D. Potter in June 1934. The suggestion that sixteen years and a World War might have outdated some of the musty old charts was brushed aside. "I believe that the rocks don't move, so what's the matter with you?"

As the price of charts rockets ever upwards—twentyfold since the fifties—the temptation to go on using old charts must be strong. In theory there is no reason why they should not be maintained up to date by small ink corrections, but they may sooner or later be overcluttered. Nevertheless at $12.25 each (1987) for a standard chart, one can sympathize with those who carry a few charts stamped "Not to be used for navigation."

When asking for one, always check the catalog number of the chart, or you may end up with one that is useless for your voyage. On the 1960 Transatlantic Race we didn't plan a stop in Newfoundland, so carried no local charts of that area. A week out of Bermuda we found ourselves heading for St. John's under jury rig. After hailing a German freighter we ended up doing a heaving-line transfer of a bottle of Scotch in return for a rolled-up chart. It was not until she was beyond recall that I found we had acquired an up-to-date chart of St. John, New Brunswick.

In case you think that was stupid, there is also a St. John's in Antigua, and others in the Red Sea and Florida, while St. John can be found in the Virgin Islands, Liberia and sou'west of Hong Kong. But I did wonder if that German knocking off our bottle of Black Label gave a moment's thought to how we were going to make a thousand miles to windward against the Gulf Stream without a mast.

If you want to cruise to Nova Scotia or the Pacific Northwest and carry all the government charts and publications you need, allowing for unscheduled stops due to weather, there will be little change out of $350, including tidal atlases and relevant pilotage books. Or, a navigator may spend $600 before a Fastnet Race, including harbor plans for every funkhole around the track. Some yacht clubs have negotiated discounts for their members which should be pursued.

Recognizing this, private chart publishers offer general charts with a substantial number of inset large-scale harbor plans. The inset harbor plans are perfectly adequate for taking a yacht in and out of harbor, but are mostly too small to lay off fixes.

The other sources of harbor plans are pilotage books. Although these mostly incorporate stern legal waivers about not being suitable for navigation except as complementary to established charts, they should not be overlooked, if only for the amount of information they give at little cost. The charts in them may be oversimplified or no more than thumbnail sketches of the port layout, but they are a lot better than nothing. Some go into immense detail, especially for those interested in rock-hopping to find quiet, barely frequented anchorages, and are more suitable for this than any recognized charts.

Sailing a 32-ft Beneteau from Cork to Hamble in March we ran into persistent strong easterlies off the Lizard and made little progress even with the motor running. Soon it was evident that we should need to put into Falmouth, Cornwall, for fuel. Our only chart was from the Lizard to Start Point on a scale 2 miles to the inch which made Falmouth look small. The scale in the *Shell Pilot* was nearly two and a half times larger, so we had no problem using it all the way to the fuel dock at the marina.

There will always be times when one has to make do with other than the official charts or publications. Bringing *Roundabout* back from Copenhagen after the 1966 World One-Ton Cup we had no intention of going through the Dutch canals, because we had only eight days to be back for Cowes Week. Somewhere off Borkum we could not do better than lay a course for the Yorkshire coast on port tack in a full W'ly gale, making painfully slow and uncomfortable progress.

There was a brief crew meeting before we were off broad-reaching for the mouth of the Ems. We had a general chart covering Helgoland to the Friesian Islands on a scale of 2 miles to the inch, but it ran out of ideas just short of Delfzijl which we knew to be port of entry to the canal linking the Ems with Zuider Zee—or Haslemere, as we soon learned to call it (Ijsselmeer). All we could get there was a Shell road map of the Netherlands. It was sufficient to get us first to Groningen for an overnight stop and then on the Lemmer at the north-eastern corner of the Ijsselmeer. Every time we met a trading barge we had to haul into the bank, which usually meant grounding in soft mud. Back in Cowes no one could figure why the spinnaker pole fittings were clogged with mud. They had been used repeatedly for punting us back into the channel.

We stopped in Lemmer long enough to watch England beat Portugal in the semifinal of the World Cup, then beat against a still sou'wester across the Ijsselmeer using a general chart of the southern North Sea. From Amsterdam down to Ijmuiden our road map did us proud. The ensuing gear-busting dead beat to windward in a succession of gales was navigated with a proper outfit of Admiralty charts and publications.

Prices of foreign charts bought in their country of origin are always significantly lower, a point to be borne in mind when ordering up for a cruise.

Chart Scales

The natural scale of charts is always printed under its title on the chart itself or alongside its reference number in the catalog. This refers to the scale at midlatitude on the area covered by the chart expressed as a ratio (e.g., 1:125,000).

To avoid buying more charts than you need, it is as well to have an idea of what these ratios mean expressed as miles or yards to the inch on the chart. The following scale is approximate, but will help to put the chart in perspective before ordering it.

Harbor plans or charts

These should ideally be 1:20,000 or larger which means lower numbers (see table, p. 10). For example, the NOAA charts for Boston (13270) and Newport, Rhode Island (13223), are both 1:20,000. This is not a hard-and-fast rule, especially for deep-

Natural Scale	Miles/yards per inch
1:5,000	140 yds to 1 in (0.07 nm)
1:10,000	275 yds to 1 in (0.14 nm)
1:15,000	400 yds to 1 in (0.2 nm)
1:20,000	550 yds to 1 in (0.275 nm)
1:50,000	1,350 yds to 1 in (0.68 nm)
1:75,000	1 nm to 1 in
1:100,000	1.4 nm to 1 in
1:150,000	2 nm to 1 in
1:300,000	4 nm to 1 in
1:500,000	6.7 nm to 1 in

water ports. There is little point in having the 1:10,000 large-scale charts of Boston Inner Harbor (13272) or Providence Harbor (13225). The latter is adequately covered for yachts by the 1:40,000 scale chart of Narragansett Bay (13221), which is a little over half a mile to the inch.

Coastal charts
It is helpful to be able to plot a passage on adjoining charts of the same scale. The NOAA has a succession of 1:80,000 charts (1.1 miles to the inch) which are ideal: four of them cover you from Indian Harbor to Buzzards Bay—Long Island Sound Western Part (12363), Long Island Sound Eastern Part (12354), Block Island Sound and Approaches (13205) and Martha's Vineyard to Block Island (13218). All of these have Loran-C position lines drawn on them.

Intracoastal waterway charts
Special charts on scale 1:40,000 (0.55 miles to the inch) cover the intracoastal waterway system along the East and Gulf Coasts.

Planning charts
These are small-scale but useful for laying off courses and distances for most of one's voyage. For example, chart 12300 issued by the Defense Mapping Agency (DMA) covers the whole 300-mile coast from Cape May to Nantucket Shoals (12300) on a scale of 1:400,000 or 5.6 miles to the inch. Or there is Cape Sable to Cape Hatteras (13003) at 16 miles to the inch.

Which Charts?
Assuming that the quality of coverage and data presentation are of equal merit, go for the charts you are accustomed to or feel comfortable with. This is more of a problem for those sailing in NW Europe, where several government and privately published charts covering the same area are available.

U.S. Charts
The standard, or conventional, charts are printed on flat, unfolded sheets of paper, 44 in × 36 in. They are issued by the National Oceanographic and Atmospheric Administration (NOAA) or, in some cases, by the Department of Defense Mapping Agency (DMA). Pocket small-craft charts are available; the conventional ones most commonly stocked by chandlers pose problems for boats without the necessary working area on their chart-table top, sometimes needing to be folded more than once. At the time of writing they all sell at $12.25 each.

Nautical Chart Catalogs can be obtained free of charge from

the Distribution Branch (N/CG 33), National Ocean Services, Riverdale, MD 20737-1149 or from major authorized dealers. They come in four parts:

1. Atlantic and Gulf Coasts, including Puerto Rico, the Virgin Islands and the Intracoastal Waterways.
2. Pacific Coast, including Hawaii, Guam and Samoa Islands.
3. Alaska, including the Aleutian Islands.
4. Great Lakes (U.S.) and adjacent waterways.

These charts are excellent, but you can be sure of finding all the buoys and beacons only on the largest-scale charts. As a result, one can be caught short for lack of detailed information, as I was when approaching the Bras d'Or Lakes in fog. The experience is painfully recalled later in this book.

Most yachtsmen on the U.S. Atlantic coast use BBA Chart Kits, which are 9 volumes of U.S. Government Charts reproduced in 22 in × 17 in format, covering from Nova Scotia to the Virgin Islands. Each has Loran-C grids and consists of a medium-scale chart covering about 100 miles of coastline, followed by a succession of larger-scale local charts, with aerial color pictures. The kits are not ideal for covering a long cruise, since you find yourself having to move from one chart to another many pages farther on. But they are good for coastal racing or cruising. Their great virtue is the 85 percent ($75) saving they represent against buying a full set of originals.

Chart symbols
All the symbols and abbreviations on U.S. charts are shown in an invaluable joint NOAA/DMA sixty-page booklet which is listed as Chart No.1 ($2.50). Besides illustrating all the symbols and notations that the navigator must know to get maximum value from each chart, it includes a glossary of terms used in hydrographic publications issued in 26 foreign countries. Color diagrams show the buoyage and other navigation aids in use in the United States and the International Association of Lighthouse Authorities (IALA) system already in use in most other countries in the world and slowly moving toward U.S. waters. The most significant notations besides those which are self-evident (such as a Maltese cross marking a church) are:

Buoys and lights are shown by a small outline depicting the type of buoy, or an abbreviated description, with a slanting purple teardrop attached to show that it is lit.

Colors in use:

Yellow	— land above the HW mark
Pale green	— foreshore which uncovers, usually overprinted "rock," "sand," "mud," etc.
Sky blue	— depths under 20 ft (3 fathoms)
Pale blue	— depths between 21 and 36 ft (6 fathoms)
White	— depths over 36 ft

Soundings and heights are mostly shown in feet at MLW, although it is assumed that a changeover to metric measurements will eventually follow the introduction of IALA conventions. The units in use are printed in bold purple letters top and bottom of each chart and also under the main title and scale.

Radio beacons and radar stations are shown within purple circles, with an abbreviated description of their function alongside.

Canadian Charts
The Canadian Hydrographic Service of the Department of Fisheries and Oceans in Ottawa issues its own catalogs of nautical charts and related publications as follows:

1. the Atlantic Coast
2. the Pacific Coast
3. the Great Lakes
4. the Arctic regions

They are obtainable free from the Department at 615 Booth Street, Ottawa, Ontario DIAOE6. Not surprisingly everything is published side by side in English and French. Each catalog contains a list of principal dealers of Canadian charts all over the world.

The charts are similar to NOAA ones, except the metric measurements for depths and heights are increasingly coming into use. Such charts are indicated by the words METRIC/ MÉTRIQUE in large magenta type on their edges.

Symbols and abbreviations are also issued in book form as Canadian Hydrographic Service Chart No. 1. The main differences to NOAA Chart No. 1 are:

The IALA buoyage system is incorporated within the section on buoys and lights.

The contour where sky blue turns to pale blue on the charts is 5 meters, 3 fathoms or 18 feet.

The glossary does not go beyond Anglo-French languages.

British Admiralty Charts

The Hydrographer of the Royal Navy and his predecessors have been at the surveying and cartography business since Captain Cook's days, longer than anyone else still in business, and should be the best. Their standard charts are delivered folded (usually only once) to 21 in × 28 in, opening out to 42 in × 28 in across. They are printed on heavy stock which survives dripping oilskins or most slopped drinks, but are soon reduced to a soggy mess if left on deck in bad weather. I always carry a zip-up clear plastic envelope big enough to accommodate an open folded chart for use on deck, for example

in negotiating a long stretch of eyeball pilotage in wet weather.

They are printed with all symbols and notations in black except for small violet teardrops making lights on buoys, or solid structures. Colored areas fall within the following conventions:

Ochre — land exposed at all times

Olive green — foreshore, banks or rocks which dry out when the tide recedes to chart datum (usually to LAT—lowest astronomical tide—not too different from Low Water Springs)

Sky blue — depths of 5 meters ($16\frac{1}{2}$ ft) or less at any tide. The next contour 10 meters (33 ft) may be outlined by a narrow blue tint showing the precise edge of the contour.

White — Water with a least depth of over 5 meters. In some cases the dividing line between blue and white may be drawn at different depths to the example just given. But a glance at the depths either side of each contour will clarify that point.

No matter how experienced you may be, always have the Admiralty publication 5011—*Symbols and Abbreviations used in Admiralty Charts*—near at hand. It is invaluable if you find yourself with a few old fathoms-and-feet charts (pre-1985) in which many of the symbols are different.

The scope of chart symbols gradually being introduced includes guidance telling visiting yachtsmen where their most common needs may be found within walking distance of landing points. The most important of these are (always shown violet or white-on-violet):

⚓ Visitors' mooring	🚩 Yacht Club
Ⓥ Visitors' Berths	⛽ Fuel
➖ Slipway	☎ Pay phone
🍺 Pub	🅿 Parking
💧 Water supply	✉ Post Office
⚓ Harbormaster's Office	⊖ Customs
⚓ Marina	🚾 Public toilets
⚓ Public Landing	🧺 Launderette

The worldwide catalog of Admiralty charts and publications (NP131) is too expensive (£10) and cumbersome to be carried in most boats, even if it was necessary. It can always be found in any chandlery or authorized chart agent, but need only be consulted if going foreign.

A small folded *Home Waters Catalogue* (NP109) can be obtained free of charge from the same source. It covers from the Arctic Circle to the Gironde, the North Sea and Skaggerak to 10°E and out to 15°W in the Western Approaches. Note, it does not cover the Baltic or Oslo Fjord. It is perfectly adequate for planning most cruises around NW Europe, excepting that the charts are listed only by their numbers, not by their title: e.g., Owers to Beachy Head is shown as a rectangular block on the South Coast, but identified only as "Chart 1652," last published in 1982, has a Decca lattice chart available and is on scale 1:75,000 (1 mile to the inch).

Corrections to charts
Corrections needed to the whole range of government charts and publications are promulgated by weekly Notices to Mariners, available free from any agent. Urgent temporary notices

may be broadcast by VHF shore radio stations, generally before their local weather forecast.

Imray Yachting Charts
These are all colored charts, generally sold in a concertina fold (like a road map) at a standard size 10¼ in × 5½ in when folded. They can also be bought unfolded (31 in × 44 in) which is 3 in bigger than the standard Admiralty chart.

The most versatile range is their C Series which cover the whole English Channel, the East Coast as far as Newcastle and the West Coast as far as Oban, but excluding the Atlantic Coast from Dingle Bay to Donegal. All the charts carry a number of harbor plans as insets. They are cheaper than the Admiralty charts, but suffer from the minor irritation when transferring from one chart to the next that adjacent charts are not always on the same scale.

There is also the "Y" series, small format for boats with limited chart table space. These are mostly unfolded at 17½ in × 25½ in but only cover inshore, estuary and harbor charts on the coast of England between Falmouth and the Wash, with one of the Isle of Man as well. They are mostly £3.95 each.

At the time of purchase, each Imray chart shows its date of issue with all the outstanding corrections needed to be made on a correction slip pasted inside the back fold. Updated correction slips can be obtained from their stockists at 20p each. Or for £2 p.a. you can get *Norrie's Bulletin of Corrections,* usually six issues a year.

Stanford Charts (Published by Barnacle Marine)
These cover the English Channel, Bristol Channel and southern North Sea in a set of nineteen small-scale charts with many large-scale harbor plans.

A list of outstanding corrections will be supplied on receipt of a stamped self-addressed envelope. The printing date of the chart should be quoted.

French Navy Charts

These are usually single fold 21 in × 29½ in, thus being wider than Admiralty charts. All their modern charts are colored, following a similar pattern to those on Admiralty charts except that the land is shown in beige, the foreshore in gray and most shades of blue to delineate shallow waters: the darker cover depths out to 5 m and then a lighter shade out to the 10 m contour.

Other points which need familiarization are:

They have no compass rose, but show a small red arrow indicating local Variation canted off a N–S longitude coordinate.

The abbreviations against light characteristics can be confusing.

Q = Quick Flashing becomes "Scint" or "Sc" on French charts.

Fl = Flashing is shown as "é."

G = Green is "V" (vert).

Part 2 of the *Shell Pilot for the English Channel* carries a useful glossary. The Admiralty List of Lights (NP74) has a comprehensive one.

Older French charts (precolor) have all their vital information in minuscule print.

The French chart service is called SHOM (Service Hydrographique et Océanographique de la Marine). They issue a free brochure catalog similar to the *Admiralty Home Waters Catalogue*, covering the coasts of France and neighboring countries—from Dunkerque to the Western Mediterranean as far as Sicily. They are of interest to foreign yachtsmen mostly for providing charts in a few places where other detailed ones do

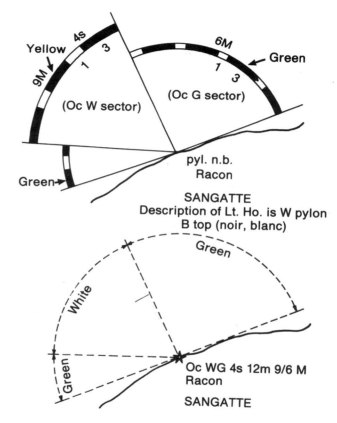

SANGATTE
Description of Lt. Ho. is W pylon
B top (noir, blanc)

SANGATTE

Same lighthouse as shown on Carte Guide (top) and Imray Charts (below)

14

not exist or are on an unsuitable scale (e.g., the Rance from Saint-Malo southward).

Carte-Guide Coastal Navigation Charts

These are full-color charts 6½ in × 12 in (when folded) covering the whole coast of France with overlapping 1:50,000 charts and larger scale harbor plans where necessary. Thus to cover Dieppe to the Alderney Race you need four charts. At this scale you need a more general chart on which to lay off and plot a course between distant points. They are printed on medium-weight paper which is billed as water-resistant.

They have their catalog on the front cover, as the Michelin road maps do.

They have their own symbols and technicolor presentation, but it is all carefully explained on each chart in French and one of four other European languages. So spend some time getting the hang of the layout and symbols, for these are outstandingly useful charts, although somewhat daunting in their proliferation of detail.

Each light shows its characteristics schematically on a radius drawn at its notional limits of visibility. The color of the light is shown yellow for a white light, otherwise they are self-evident. The eclipse (i.e., dark) period is left blank. The timing of each cycle is shown in minuscule figures around the radius of the light's visibility giving the precise timing of the flashes (see p. 14).

There is a 360°True and magnetic compass rose, and close inshore tidal current arrows and a fascinating compass presentation of the incidence, direction and strengths of the observed winds during April to September.

All the buoys and beacons are shown large enough to save having to turn to the IALA system diagram to identify them. A whistle buoy is marked "SS" on French charts.

The land is shown pale yellow with all the roads correctly designated by number (N130, D524, etc.). These charts score over others by the extent of the information they give about what can be seen inland from seaward.

Drying-out foreshore is shown in bright yellow for sand or as rose clusters for rocks. The blue tint goes out to the 3 meters depth contour.

The scale of their harbor plans tends to be too small for comfort.

These charts are available in any Librairie Maritime. A stamped addressed envelope to their publishers will get the corrections. Mercifully, corrections to French charts are needed much less frequently than those covering U.K. waters.

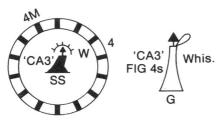

Carte Guide System for Fl G 4s with 4M range. G "spokes" show 1 sec G flash after 3 secs eclipse

Same buoy as shown on Imray Chart

Gnomonic Charts

These are constructed with all the meridians of longitude meeting at the poles. They are commonly found in atlases depicting Antarctica or the seas north of Spitzbergen and the

Bering Strait. Their practical use for yacht navigators is to determine the Great Circle (GC) course and distance on a long passage in comparatively high latitudes. If you are planning a GC route from Bermuda to the Scillies, lay off a straight line on the gnomonic chart from St. David's Head to the Bishop Rock and take a succession of course readings as the line crosses the meridians 10° apart. You will set sail on 050° and make your landfall 2,760 miles later steering 088°.

Mercatorial Plots

All charts in normal use are constructed on Mercator's projection wherein the longitudes are always at right angles to the parallels of latitude. The price to be paid for this convenience is that the latitude scale at either side of the chart is the only one giving the correct distances. For ocean passages it is desirable to have mercatorial plotting sheets in which the latitudes are numbered, but the degrees of longitude can be marked by the navigator to cover wherever he happens to be sailing. They are obtainable on both sides of the Atlantic covering up to 10° of latitude and longitude. But it is easy enough to construct your own, either by using a calculator to solve the equation that 1° of latitude is drawn on a plot for, say, 45°N or S as secant 45°. Or it can be constructed by marking off your desired longitude scale, drawing a line at 45° to it from one end, then ruling off a series of perpendicular lines. Where they cut the oblique 45° line you can measure the latitude scale along that line (see diagram on right).

Oceanic plotting sheets are available on a scale of 1:250,000 (3.4 nm to the inch) in 6° bands of latitude. Thus 48°—54° is Admiralty Chart 5437. There are corresponding U.S. mercatorial plotting sheets. Sheets for plotting at a much greater scale, complete with their own compass rose, are obtainable for plotting out celestial observations.

A mercatorial plot is essential if you find that the ordinary

To construct a mercatorial plotting sheet using any convenient longitude scale

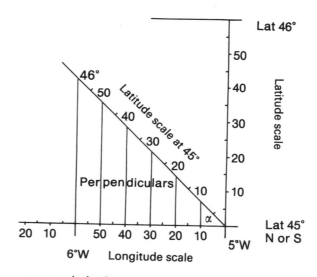

α = angle in degrees from horizontal corresponding to latitude

charts for your track are on too small a scale and will not permit accurate EP plotting. This is the case on the Bermuda Race.

Manuals and publications

If you are not planning to go far afield, all you need to supplement the information on your charts are local tide tables. These are often listed in the local newspapers, on radio and

16

BOSTON, Massachusetts Approximate time of tides according to state of moon.

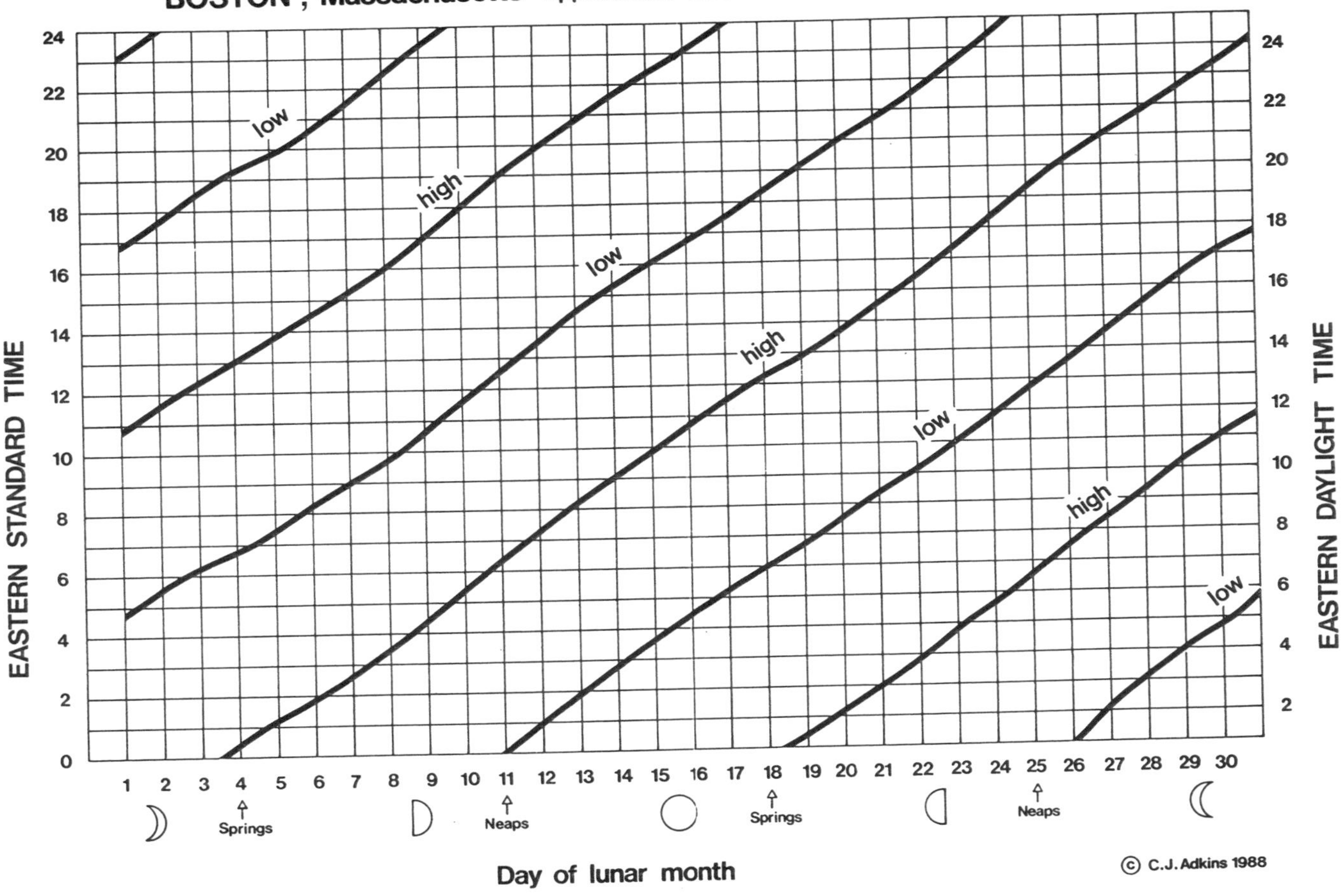

EASTERN STANDARD TIME
0
2
4
6
8
10
12
14
16
18
20
22
24
EASTERN DAYLIGHT TIME
low
high
low
high
low
high
low
1 2 3 4 5 6 7 8 9 10 11 12 13 14 15 16 17 18 19 20 21 22 23 24 25 26 27 28 29 30
Springs
Neaps
Springs
Neaps
Day of lunar month
© C.J. Adkins 1988

provided free at chandleries or marina offices. There are many pilotage books, tidal atlases and almanacs giving much fuller information, such as the annual *Eldridge Tide and Pilot Book* or *Reed's Almanac* covering from Nova Scotia to Key West. For the greatest detail refer to the following NOAA publications:

U.S. Coast Pilots, in 9 volumes. Numbers 1 to 4 cover the Eastern seaboard; number 5, the Gulf of Mexico, Puerto Rico and the Virgin Islands; number 6 covers the Great Lakes; number 7 covers the whole West Coast and Hawaii.

Tide Tables. One volume covers the East Coast of North and South America; another covers the West Coast and the Hawaiian Islands, with the rest of the world published separately.

Tidal Current Charts. These are available for most harbors and bays in which tides play a significant part.

Standard Ports

Certain ports are listed from which the times and heights of tides for all other ports can be extrapolated. The most important of these on the Eastern seaboard is Boston, from which can be derived all data for over 170 other ports, as far afield as the Carolinas and Florida. Harbors that are reasonably close to Boston, say between Portsmouth and Cape Cod, have negligible time differences. Bridgeport, Connecticut, is also close to Boston tide times, whereas Newport, Rhode Island, is 3¼ hours ahead and Sandy Hook, New Jersey, is 2½ hours after Boston. So, if you remember that Boston has HW Springs at about 12:30 EST, two to three days after a full moon, you can make a useful approximation without reference to tide tables. The smallest ones (Neaps) occur a week either side of Springs soon after the first and last quarters of the moon. As a rough guide the time of HW is 40 minutes later each day: thus three days after Springs it will be two hours later, and so on. See Adkins Tide Ready Reckoner (see p. 17). Except for areas like the Bay of Fundy and Alaska, tidal ranges are rarely over 10 feet, with the difference between Springs and Neaps usually only 3—4 feet. Note that for certain bottleneck channels through which the tidal current runs at high speed (Pollock Rip, the Race and Hell Gate) the tables give the times at which the currents turn from ebb to flood, which may differ significantly from the times of HW or LW. While the tidal ranges are not great, the effect they have on tidal currents is significant. As a rough rule the current velocity at Neaps will be 60 percent of that shown for Springs, prorating for tides in between.

Light Lists

If you want the full lists of lights, giving all their data for whatever area you may be sailing to, both the Admiralty and NOAA give worldwide coverage in a series of different volumes, with corrections issued in *Weekly Notices to Mariners*. The Coast Guard also publishes its own 7-volume series of light lists covering the whole U.S. coastline and offlying islands. For day-to-day, use the extracts given in *Reed's* or *Eldridge*.

Chart table rack for pencils, dividers, compass rubber

Magnifying glass with light

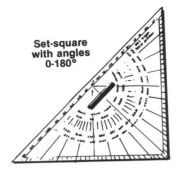

Set-square with angles 0-180°

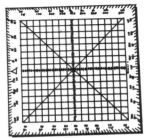

0-360° protractor for use by alignmen to lat or long

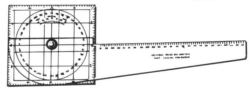

Protractors aligned to lat or long lines as datum

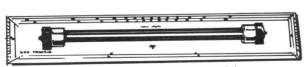

Lattice parallel ruler (seldom room for operation)

Parallel rulers (unstable in a yacht)

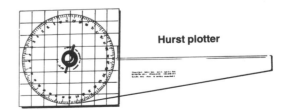

Hurst plotter

19

Plotting and other basic nav-aids

Pencil (B or 2B).

Eraser soft white rubber.

Dividers preferably robust brass ones with steel tips, about 6—8 in long, preferably those that can be opened and closed with one hand. These should be stowed vertically, near at hand to the chart working surface. Spares for all of them should be in a separate drawer, together with a pencil sharpener (maxi-yachts go for electrically operated pencil sharpeners, but you might go so far as to have the type which collects its own shavings in a screw-on cartridge). In the same drawer should be the navigator's pencil, flashlight and spare spectacles—or a magnifying glass. Also lens papers for cleaning binoculars.

Parallel ruler or protractor There is a wide variety available. The most unsuitable for yachts are the traditional ones: either those which have their own rollers built-in or those which open and shut on swinging lattice arms which enable you to transfer a bearing from a compass rose to the required point on the chart, or vice versa, by a maddening crab-walk. Those heavy old brass roller parallel rulers are dangerous in a small boat. They are liable to slip while being used, or run out of chart surface to move on.

There are several satisfactory protractors which have a rotating arm about the center of a square grid, any of whose verticals can be aligned to a meridian or horizontals to an E—W latitude coordinate. You set the center of the protractor over the point from which a bearing is to be laid off and swing the arm to the 0—360° reading desired. The line can then be drawn on the straight edge of the plotting arm. Some of these also can have the Variation screwed in as a fixed correction. Of these the Hurst Protractor may be the most popular (see p. 19).

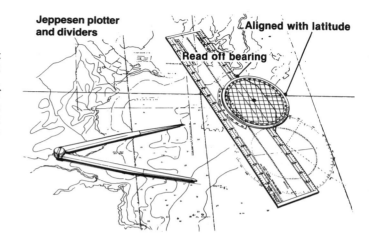

Jeppesen plotter and dividers / **Aligned with latitude** / **Read off bearing**

Some navigators use right-angle set-squares, sliding them along a straight surface, but they also depend on nothing slipping during the chartwork.

In the early sixties I was taking part in the Miami-Nassau powerboat race, when I met the winner of the Powderpuff Derby (Grannies racing light aircraft across the United States). She introduced me to the Jeppesen plotter PJ1, which is so far superior to any other yacht protractor that I never travel without one. It is only 13 in × 5½ in, is easily stowed, simple to line up to any bearing (magnetic or True) and retains its alignment to any coordinate by friction alone. So it is ideal for transferring courses or bearings from one chart to another. More importantly, it is the fastest plotter afloat.

The standard article is marketed from Englewood, Colorado, has a scale of statute miles to light aircraft requirements (1:1,500,000), but I have superimposed a scale 1:150,000 at mid-latitude 50° for U.K. use. Obtainable from suppliers of air navigation maps and instruments. The U.K. equivalent is the Airtour Navigation Plotter (ANZP1).

Clocks

A ship's clock is also a necessity. Nowadays most sailors have quartz wristwatches, some with digital readout in hours, minutes and seconds, although they seem to be going out of fashion. I have a 1960 waterproof analog Ingersoll with a resetting stopwatch which is also invaluable in, for example, timing light characteristics. I keep an old Rolex Oyster set on GMT as a spare. The old days of a gimballed chronometer in a brass-bound mahogany case, with the deck watch error (DWE) recorded daily, are gone forever.

They have left me with one abiding memory—losing the 1969 Fastnet in *Crusade* by 68 seconds on corrected time after unsuccessfully protesting the Race Committee for taking the elapsed time five minutes in error. We recorded the finishing time on board from our chronometer a few minutes after it had been checked against the BBC pips for 0900. All the finishing times were noted by a dockyard employee in the Breakwater Fort from a wall clock with an unsynchronized sweep second hand. Watching from the lawn of Admiralty House was the Flag Officer himself, already late for an 0900 meeting. As soon as he saw our saffron spinnaker drop, he noted the time on his wristwatch, for which he later showed the jury that he had kept its daily error from the 0800 time signal every day for the last three months.

Nevertheless the protest was thrown out, which was hardly surprising. The night before the Protest Committee convened, one of the hierarchy of the RORC chanced to meet the Flag Officer Plymouth, without realizing who he was, since he was in plain clothes. The Admiral was assured that *Crusade* would not be allowed to win the Fastnet on a protest, no matter how strong the evidence in her favor.

The winner had not been reported around the Bishop Rock 98 miles away when we secured alongside Mount Wise, so had to average better than 7 kts to win. She did.

It happened to be my birthday. The Admiral's present to me was the current synoptic weather chart. Between Plymouth and the Lizard there was a beautiful col—a zone of no pressure differential with theoretically no wind at all.

Later it was found that both boats had raced under incorrect ratings, to the extent that the finishing time could have been recorded over an hour wrong without depriving us of the Fastnet. But that is another story.

Binoculars

These, as an aid to the legendary MkI Eyeball, are also on the must list. There is no sensible choice other than rubber-bonded 7 × 50s with individual eyepiece focusing. The 7 describes the power magnification: the 50 is the field of view in mm. Chandleries will offer 8 × 30 or even 10 × 70, but the pedigree of the 7 × 50 is unanswerable. In World War II most of the navies of the world started with different-sized binoculars, but all ended with 7 × 50s. They are the optimum compromise between being able to spot a target and hold it steady enough from a heaving platform. Some incorporate an illuminated bearing compass.

Depth sounders

Although it is often useful to be able to read depths of over 30 fathoms, as for picking up the Labadie Bank on the way back from the Fastnet, say, most yachtsmen primarily want to know how close they are to grounding in shoal water.

The traditional method of heaving a lead is no longer practical or desirable while underway (imagine the chaos of catching the blooper on the let-go), but it remains an unanswerable check against an electronic echo sounder with the boat at rest, even if your lead line consists of a winch handle tied onto a spare sheet.

Crewing in RCODs on the Crouch or X-boats in Chichester Harbor we had a stout bamboo cane marked to a length one foot more than the draft of the boat. On orders this dipstick was pushed down on the lee side. A touch meant lee-oh. For small workboats or fishing dayboats I see no harm in that.

But most boats have an electronic echo sounder pinging through a transducer in the hull with a remote reading display over the chart table and/or on deck. There are many brands on offer. This is an area where you tend not to get your money's worth, in that some of the cheaper models are better than their more prestigious competitors. A demonstration afloat is the only answer. Find out:

(a) the datum of the depth displayed: e.g., is it measuring from the waterline? the bottom of the keel? or the depth from the transducer to the bottom?

It is usually the last, but check. Zero-point on the display can be adjusted to suit. Then have a Dyno strip glued alongside the echo-sounder display saying "We ground at 1.8 m (6 ft) on the clock." Most owners feel comfortable with the actual depth of water displayed, since that is what is on the chart.

A few years ago I went on a blind date navigating an Admiral's Cup boat. Going out from Cowes to the start of the first inshore race I asked where the echo sounder measured from. No one knew, so the owner abruptly altered to put the boat aground on the Shrape where we could verify the matter by noting the difference between the draft and the depth on the echo sounder. There was a sluicing ebb tide, so I advised against that plan, thus narrowly avoiding watching the race from a mud berth.

(b) The behavior of the display in shallow water.

Sometimes it flicks back and forth just when you most need an unambiguous steady reading. Tuning the gain does not always calm it down.

(c) Whether false echoes, like shoals of fish, show up for what they are.

There are all kinds of fancy warning devices on offer, like a hooter to sound off before you ground at anchor on a falling tide. But none is better than the instrument's ability to interpret the raw data.

What present-day yachts' echo sounders will *not* do is warn you that you are about to hit an underwater obstruction or sudden steep shelving. So it's of little use short-tacking along a beach with rocky outcrops. Nor was there any warning for single-handed circumnavigator Desmond Hampton when *Gipsy Moth V* piled on to an island in the Bass Strait while he slept.

There's no substitute for having a good look at the exposed rocks and foreshore at Low Water Springs and noting your own safe transits. Other people's local knowledge can only be evaluated by trial and error. Uffa Fox often frightened me by urging Max Aitken to take his big wishbone schooner *Lumberjack* ever closer inshore in a foul tide. At one spot his confidence was based on having ridden his mare, Frantic, off the beach and out of her depth at that point. Suddenly we came up all-standing at 10 knots. "We must have drawn more than 16 hands," was Max's historic comment.

Even apparently up-to-date charts will not be 100 percent guarantee if depended upon for the last couple of feet under the keel. Approach channels shift, for example, in the Nantucket Shoals area; harbor entrances silt up; underwater obstructions may not always be marked on the chart (Remember the two top British 1985 Admiral's Cup boats which hit the same submerged wreck? One of them sank.); unusually low tides can occur after a prolonged blow from one direction.

Once I was having a late lunch at Chausey with Marin-Marie the great French marine artist whose flagstaff in front of his waterside home always flew an RORC burgee as an invitation to members dropping anchor there. We had to pick up a crew member at St. Helier at a fixed time, so I was anxious to be away. Our host persuaded me to stop for another cognac. The time lost would be recovered by having the local lifeboat coxswain tow us out through the more direct but narrow North channel. Four hours later we were able to walk back to the Hotel du Fort et des Îles for an early dinner, as cows grazed around our keel.

The RORC's log of *Griffin II* on a Morgan Cup Race in 1957 describes how she won the race on a moonless night by short-tacking along the front at Brighton closer inshore than her rivals, cheating the tide. The moment to tack and stand off was not called from the echo sounder. Instead a crewman on the pulpit hurled an empty bottle ahead as far as he could. If it was heard to hit the shingle on the beach it was time to go about. The race was also memorable when Slushie the Cook was caught washing his underpants in the pressure cooker, having first flashed up the Primus using liqueur brandy instead of methylated spirits. Both worked well—for him.

In bigger boats some go for a stylus display on a moving paper reel, which plots out the shape of the bottom, but is hardly worth the space it takes up.

Of all the modern aids to navigation the echo sounder remains the least reliable and therefore the one most in need of a corroborative check at any opportunity.

The moral of all these frightening stories of unexpected grounding is that the cruising yachtsman need never put them to the test. Keep outside the 2-fathom (or 3 m) line unless you are in a well-buoyed channel and have some idea of the height of the tide above the chart datum. For all practical purposes this is Low Water Springs.

Predicting depths

To find out what depth of water there will be at a given time and day in any port, first determine the range of the tides there. This is simply the difference between the heights above datum at HW and LW.

(1) Look up the heights above datum for high and low water, Springs and Neaps in local tide tables, or by looking up the nearest standard port in the almanacs. Take Philadelphia:

At Springs MHW	7.2 ft		At Neaps	5.7 ft
MLW	−0.2 ft			0.6 ft
Range	7.4			5.1

The difference is only 2.3 ft, so might be considered negligible, as it is almost everywhere in North American waters except in the Bay of Fundy.

(2) Then apply the "Twelfths Rule" which states that for each successive hour after LW the tide will rise as follows (in twelfths of the range):

$$1 - 2 - 3 - 3 - 2 - 1.$$

So, if the tide is shown to have a range of 7.4 ft, as above, and you want to know how far it will have fallen three and one half hours after HW: first hour $\frac{1}{12}$ = 0.6 ft; second hour $\frac{2}{12}$ = 1.2 ft; third hour $\frac{3}{12}$ = 1.9; next thirty minutes = 0.9, making 4.6 ft in all, so that it will then be only 2.8 ft above LW. Incidentally, the progression from Springs heights to Neaps is one-seventh per day.

These are only approximations and do not apply where there are double High Waters. For these you should work your way through the prediction-method in the Admiralty form NP159, the curves within almanac tides tables, or rely on locally published tables. No system exists to be more precise after the wind has been blowing strongly for a week in the same direction except to ask the local harbormaster.

Speed and distance log

For any displacement powerboat or yacht under auxiliary power with her sails furled the simplest way of judging speed made good (Vmg) through the water is to know the rev-knot ratio of the motor. It is usually a straight-line relationship (e.g., at 2,000 rpm you will be making 7 kts, 1,500 rpm is $5\frac{1}{4}$ kts and 1,000 rpm $3\frac{1}{2}$ kts). The amount to add or subtract for tidal current is a matter of looking up the relevant tidal information for the place and time of day. Then there is an allowance to be made for windage.

For example, if the chart tells you there should be 1.3 kts favorable current and you are motoring before a stiff breeze, make a judgment on how fast you would be going with no motor at all. Unless it is a gale of wind, it is unlikely to be over a knot on top of the tide. Let's say 2 kts for tide and wind. The rev-knot ratio says 6 kts, so you should be making 8 kts over the ground. How much to allow for windage is a matter of observation based on experience of the boat. It is a simple matter to check by timing a run between two known points and working out the distance run, using a calculator or looking it up in a speed-time-distance table. There is a simple formula for doing this without either: the distance a ship runs in hundreds of yards in three minutes is its speed in knots, so that 900 yds in three minutes or 300 yds in one minute both mean 9 kts. This can also be expressed as:

$$\text{Speed in knots} = \frac{\text{distance in yards}}{\text{time in seconds}} \times 1.8$$

$$\text{or:} \quad = \frac{\text{distance in miles}}{\text{time in minutes}} \times 60$$

$$\text{or:} \quad = \frac{\text{distance in feet}}{10 \times \text{time in seconds}} \times 6$$

The last lends itself to calculating the speed by using a Dutchman's log, which is by timing how long it takes your boat to sail her own length. The classic way of doing this is to have someone in the pulpit with a few empty beer cans and another in the taffrail with a stopwatch. The first one throws a can out ahead of the boat and far enough out to avoid hitting the hull. As it passes him he drops his hand. The man aft then times the can as it passes the taffrail. This should be repeated to get a mean reading. Thus, sailing a 40 ft boat, if a beer can is timed to take four seconds to pass down its overall length her speed is:

$$\frac{40 \times 6}{4 \times 10} = 6 \text{ kts}$$

Another aid to judging speed through the water is to use a formula developed by RAF photoreconnaissance aircraft for measuring ships' speeds. The square root of the distance in feet from the stem to the point where the *second* bow wave shows against the hull × 1.4 is its speed in knots. With modern yachts this also defines hull speed (up to the threshold of planing), for the second bow wave is at the transom and holding the boat in a formula:

$$\text{Hull speed} = 1.4\sqrt{\text{length of wetted surface}}$$

Thus a boat 36 ft long has a theoretical maximum hull speed of $1.4 \times \sqrt{36} = 1.4 \times 6 = 8.4$ kts.

In calm seas the position of the second bow wave against the ship's side is clearly seen from on deck. Say the shrouds are 16 ft abaft the stem and the leading edge of the cockpit 25 ft. Then the second bow wave abreast these points would be 1.4×4 (5.6 kts) and 1.4×5 (7 kts) respectively. The beauty of this method is that errors of estimating the distance abaft the stem are square-rooted.

Experienced sailors looking over the side can make a fair guess at the speed of a yacht, probably correct to ±1 kt. Powerboats are more difficult, but their shaft rpm/kt ratio is more reliable than any other *ad hoc* method.

I am not suggesting that a log is not one of the Bare Necessities, but simply recalling an era before the advent of reliable hull-mounted logs when Erroll Bruce and Adlard Coles persuaded us after their epic Transatlantic Race in 24-ft sloops

that the drag of a towed log over that distance could add eight and one-half hours to the elapsed time of a 6-kt passage even if it only slowed you down by 0.1 kt. So for the next few seasons many RORC navigators kept their towed logs inboard and used variations of the methods spelled out above.

On balance I believe a reliable log is a highly desirable comfort to the navigator. Some, like the Walker towed log, primarily reel off distance run. The paddle wheel or impeller type, like B & G, primarily read speed. But either can be used as the prime source for giving the other dimension on a remote analog or digital display.

Towed logs are appreciably cheaper than any electronic models. The correct way to stream one is to pay out the inboard end of the rope first, so as to get all the kinks out of it. Then recover it hand over hand, hook on and let the spinner trail aft. The snags are:

(a) Some fish take them as bait, usually snapping the line. So you must carry a spare.

(b) You must remember to hand the log before entering harbor or shoal water, before going astern on the motor, or towing a dinghy or crossing another yacht astern.

(c) Unless you have a remote reading dial, you have to get to the taffrail to take readings.

(d) They can be fouled by weed, especially in tropical waters. Or they can snag a J-cloth or other gash finding its way overboard.

There is also available an electronic trailing log which does not spin on its own towline, but transmits the rotation of a helical impeller as speed and distance to analog dials inboard.

Impeller logs are extremely accurate, provided they have been calibrated, adjusted and checked to lie in the same plane as the water flowing under the hull. After calibration by checking over a measured distance in tideless conditions (or by taking the average of runs in reciprocal directions), the display reading

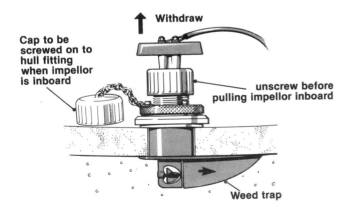

Withdraw

Cap to be screwed on to hull fitting when impellor is inboard

unscrew before pulling impellor inboard

Weed trap

25

for speed and distance can be adjusted by a thumbscrew on the back of the display console. My general experience is that it pays not to adjust the log unless you have piled up a mass of evidence in favor of doing so. Then do it in very small steps.

The location of impellers can be critical, so it is as well to take technical advice from the suppliers if you are fitting one for the first time. You want it to be in undisturbed water flow, free from surface aeration or coming clear of the water when pitching. In bigger boats it is the practice to fit two impellers, with a gravity switch changing from port to starboard automatically on tacking.

To adjust for optimum reading, slack off the cap locking the log and have someone watch on the display unit to see what happens when you slew the impeller slowly from 15° off centerline, through fore and aft to 15° off the other way. When the reading peaks at highest speed, lock the impeller. It will not always be precisely in the fore-and-aft line, especially if the hull mounting is off center. With two impellers you find that both are toed slightly inwards. This is a very sensitive adjustment.

Likewise it is important to have the impeller pushed downwards to its full extent.

Although modern impeller logs have much improved fore-and-aft weedguards, they are still prone to pick up foreign bodies. On sailing into kelp or a cluster of *Sargassum* weed, trouble soon manifests itself, as the log suddenly stops recording.

Last summer I gathered a collector's item 20 miles south of Anvil Point. The log was stopped by a condom of such heroic proportions that we had a lively debate whether it had come overboard from a Russian or American ship. But even fine strands of weed can wrap themselves in the bearing of the impeller and slow it down, so that the boat speed may drop only imperceptibly, giving rise to sidelong glances at the helmsman or talk of a sail change.

In either case the remedy is the same—an awkward, wet job for the navigator. First the sailbags and off-watch oilskins have to be yanked clear before the impeller can be withdrawn into the boat and the hull-fitting shut off by screwing its cap on. Fine weed is best removed by a pin. To check that it is clear, puff at the impeller to be sure it is spinning freely and activating the display dial. If it whizzes round and does not show on the dial, you have a real problem—maybe a fault in the cable run.

But it may be more serious. Ten days out from the Canaries in a Swan "47," rolling along the 17th parallel in a steady 25 kt breeze from the quarter against a blue-and-white backdrop of breaking seas and marching cumulus, we celebrated our furthest point from land with a tot of Fundador. We were nowhere near any shipping lane and hadn't seen anything but seabirds and flying fish for over a week. Suddenly there was a loud bang. A whale or a submerged oil drum perhaps? Then a 4 in plank about 10 ft long surfaced in our wake. To be more precise, two 5 ft planks did, neatly bisected by a karate chop from our stem. The log now read zero. Both impellers had been sheared off clean, weedguards and all. No more flotsam was seen, then or for the rest of the trip, so we must have picked up a solitary paint-ship plank which could have fallen overboard off Lisbon or Bantry Bay.

Paddlewheel Logs Most logs these days are of the paddlewheel variety, which are less prone to be fouled by weed. Their installation should follow the same guidelines as for impeller logs.

The Sonic Log A new log which defies all underwater debris because its two sensors are flush-fitted to the hull is the Brookes & Gatehouse sonic log. This measures the difference

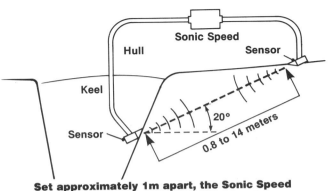

Sonic Speed

Hull

Sensor

Keel

Sensor

20°

0.8 to 14 meters

Set approximately 1m apart, the Sonic Speed transducers operate outside the boundary layer on the centerline of the boat

between the speed of sound at rest and that at any boat speed, by averaging out the different timing of signals pulsing alternately fore and aft.

The location of the transducers is critical: on the centerline not less than 2 ft 6 in (0.8 m) or more than 4 ft 6 in (1.4 m) apart and set at an angle of 20°—30° below the horizontal. This requirement makes the log suitable only for boats with fin keels. The usual arrangement is to have the forward transducer about 3 ft forward of the point of attachment of the keel to the hull and the after one 2 ft down its leading edge. For measuring speed through the water it seems to be the complete answer.

Other means of measuring speed and distance run Most of the hyperbolic aids (Decca, Loran-C, for example) have built-in computers which will provide all the speed-and-distance answers by working out solutions between successive fixes. But they

have their own aberrations which will be discussed later in the book. Even farther out of reach for yachtsmen because of cost and/or weight are certain military toys, like the Global Position System—a continuous-fixing Sat-Nav—or the Inertial Navigation System as fitted in nuclear submarines. There is also the eternal dream of a doppler log which will give course and speed made good over the seabed. But no one has yet cracked that as a practical proposition for yachtsmen.

The Bare Necessities—Good Enough for Suhaili On his epic 27,000 mile solo circumnavigation lasting 313 days in 1968/9, Robin Knox-Johnston managed on:

- a magnetic compass of the same type as fitted in a ship's lifeboat, with an old ex-Service hand-bearing compass as standby
- a hand lead line
- celestial navigation tables and an old sextant whose mirrors were soon blotched by seawater
- a windup chronometer depending for its credibility on time signals from his radio
- only thirteen Admiralty charts, because he couldn't afford more even in those far-off days when they cost half a guinea each. Some of them were stamped "Not to be used for navigation"
- parallel rulers, dividers and pencils
- a towed log, which he gave up using after it was fouled in the Doldrums by gooseneck barnacles, which look like toothpaste and cling like limpets; he made over 20,000 miles without a log

More recently Dr. Marvin Creamer has made a leisurely circumnavigation in a 35 ft boat without any navigation aids whatever—not even a clock—and won the CCA's 1985 Blue Water Medal for it, but that merely demonstrates what Drake and Magellan had to do, not what is recommended for you. Dr. Creamer knew he'd rounded the Horn by hitting neither the land nor the ice. Polynesian navigators made some astonishing long ocean voyages without any instruments (for none existed). Mostly they relied on knowing when a particular star rose or set over their target; but they could read many other signs, such as cloud formations, birds heading for an atoll, the direction of the swell and the seawater temperature. They did not claim to fly by the seat of their pants, but by a homing device in their testicles.

Even in the smallest yachts I hold that space and thought devoted to providing the navigator with an efficiently designed and equipped chart table will pay dividends. In today's parlance this tends to be called "the nav-station," but it means the same thing: a corner where the navigator can do his work with the least distraction and yet within easy communication of the helmsman.

If you are buying a stock boat you have to take what is already installed and then fit in all the navigator's aids to his best advantage.

If you are building or converting then you might do better. The following considerations apply:

(a) *Location* In a powerboat with a cabin there is no problem: the chart table should be a working surface next to the wheel facing for'ard. The worst chart table I ever endured was the attack-plot in an "H" Class submarine (vintage 1916). When the attack team was closed up, my station was sitting inside the head, with the door shut and its upper panel pulled down on to my knees as the plotting surface. Once, I left the tools of my trade elsewhere, so the straight edge of a toothbrush handle was conscripted as a substitute for dividers and protractors. It seemed to work, but luckily it was not in the face of the enemy.

In a yacht without a wheelhouse there are many options. My worst memories center on the Ron Holland Two-Tonner *Knockout*, when the chart table was set fore and aft against the

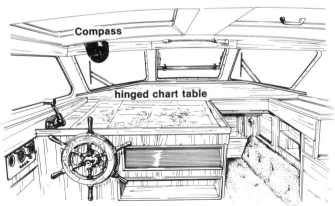

No frills on this single screw powerboat

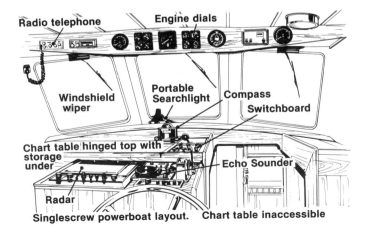

Singlescrew powerboat layout. Chart table inaccessible

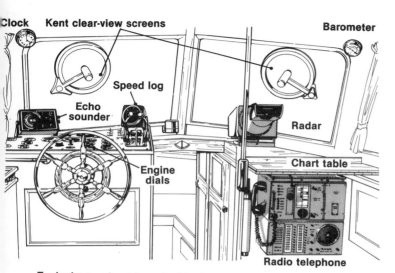

Clock   Kent clear-view screens   Barometer

Speed log

Echo
sounder   Radar

Engine   Chart table
dials

                                                 Radio telephone

Typical powerboat layout with chart table folded out of use

ship's side, opposite the galley—some distance from the hatch leading to the cockpit. On one tack the working surface was far below me and heeled away at 25°. On the other there was little to stop everything ending up in the galley bilge. On top of that, the cabin sole had to be kept clear for stowing sailbags amidships and for moving them when required. So the navigator's seat was a round stool top on a swinging arm which could be stowed out of the way under the chart table.

That experience need not rule out a fore-and-aft chart table altogether. For example if you have a narrow shoal-draft boat with a high centerboard casing dividing the available space

below in half, there may be no alternative. Such is the case in a Freedom 34 which John Oakeley swears by (see p. 31). He has deliberately put his chart table well forward and away from the hatch so as to keep sea and rain off his electronics. In practical terms most electronic nav-aids are in splash-proof consoles, so the principal sufferers from water coming down the hatch are the charts and the navigator himself.

A fore-and-aft table is also acceptable in any boat which is designed to be sailed upright, like a multihull. Otherwise the choice must be overwhelmingly for an athwartships working surface near the after hatch.

In *Toscana* (ex-*Blizzard*, the Frers "51" IOR prototype) the chart table was once amidships, permitting the navigator the luxury of a tilting seat which could be locked at an angle when the boat was heeled. Not so good for short-tacking. The trouble with this arrangement was that anything not nailed down to the table had two ways in which to go when the boat gave a lurch.

So we end up with the solution most often found in stock boats: a nav-station built out from the ship's side with the after cabin bulkhead forming the backrest to the navigator's seat.

The all-time best nav-station for me was in the 48-ft Illingworth & Primrose cutter *Outlaw*. The navigator worked facing aft, with a rectangular port at eye level through which he could communicate with the helmsman, since the wheel was on the bulkhead at the for'ard end of the cockpit. The helmsman could look straight down onto his chart, while the navigator and skipper both had quarter-berths in the after cabin, shut off from the rest of the boat (see p. 32).

(b) *Vital Statistics* The working surface of the chart table should be at least big enough to take a government chart without double-folding or too much overlap, say 30 in × 22 in. The navigator's seat should have 18 in lateral clearance abaft the table, with a bench height of 19 in and a least

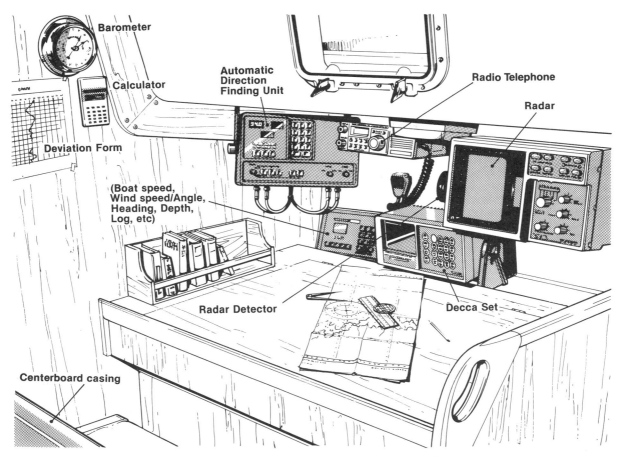

Barometer

Calculator

Deviation Form

Automatic
Direction
Finding Unit

Radio Telephone

Radar

(Boat speed,
Wind speed/Angle,
Heading, Depth,
Log, etc)

Radar Detector

Decca Set

Centerboard casing

A connoisseur's Nav-Station in a centerboard "Freedom"

31

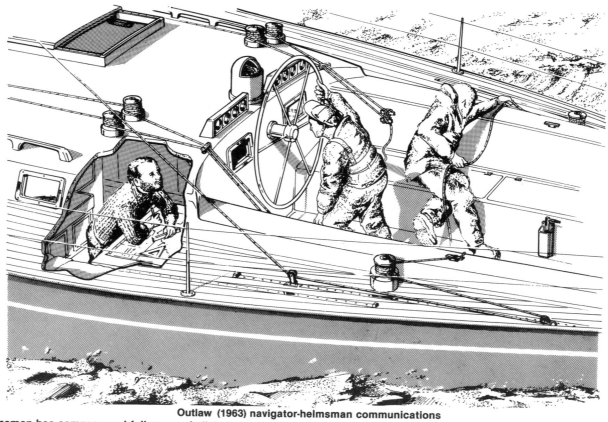

Outlaw (1963) navigator-helmsman communications
Helmsman has compass and full range of dials in front of him. All sail trimming is abaft him and does not distract.

clearance under the bottom of the chart table structure of 8 in. The lid of the chart table should be hinged at its forward end with a least depth of 4 in of stowage under it. Thus the ideal height of the chart table working surface should be 32 in. The top should be flat and contained within the fiddles 1 in proud on each side; across its after side either a ½-in fiddle or provision for spring-steel clips to hold the chart in position. The lid should be hinged so as to open to at least 45° and be held there either by an overhead shockcord or by a prop.

Under one end of the chart stowage there should be a drawer not less than 4 in × 4 in, sectioned to accommodate the spare pencils, rubbers, pencil sharpener, stopwatch, the keys for locking up the boat, a mini-flashlight and lens cleaning paper.

The open end of the navigator's seat must be provided with a click-on safety harness strong enough to take his full weight when heeled.

(c) *Lighting* All the boat's lighting down below should ideally have red or white optional bulbs, preferably of the type activated by three-way toggle switches. Additionally the chart table should have its own flexible finger light so arranged that it can, if need be, illuminate the inside of the chart table when its lid is open. Red lighting below should be the norm for the crew, but the navigator must have the luxury of a white finger light for chartwork, provided it does not catch the helmsman's eye.

During the Transatlantic Race in 1960 in *Drumbeat* we got dismasted around the change of the watch at midnight. At the cry for "all hands on deck" all the cabin lighting was switched on—white. As they stumbled out on deck one or two of the crew nearly went straight over the side, reaching for guardwires which were no longer there. They were not acclimatized to night vision, as they would have been if they had rolled out of their racks into red lighting.

Tools of the trade There must be secure stowages for pen-

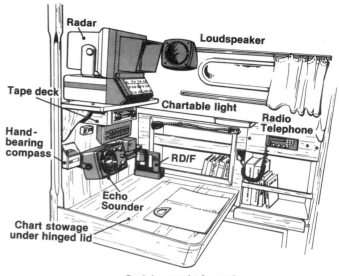

Cruising yacht lay out

cils, dividers, parallel ruler or protractor, a rubber, the navigator's spectacles (or a magnifying glass) and the almanacs or tables in use.

The last needs a bookrack capable of holding publications 11 in × 8 in, so arranged that they don't fly out at any angle of heel. It should be 18 in long, but can be split into two.

Inside the chart table the charts needed for the passage should be placed in the order in which they are going to be used, with a small-scale general chart of the whole voyage on top. All the rest of the charts should be stowed elsewhere,

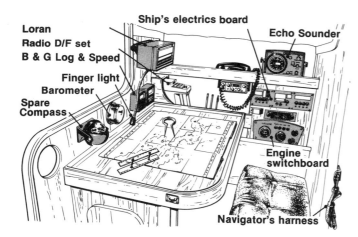

Nav-Station in a First "32"

Loran
Radio D/F set
B & G Log & Speed

Ship's electrics board

Echo Sounder

Finger light
Barometer

Spare
Compass

Engine
switchboard

Navigator's harness

Hand-bearing compass
Binoculars
D/F antenna and headset
Sextant

Also located so that the navigator can see or operate them without moving should be:

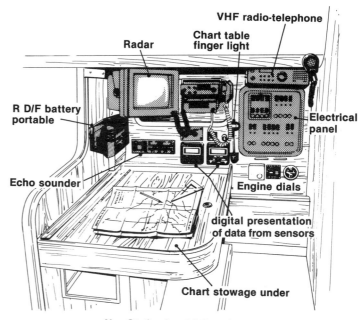

Nav-Station in a 34-ft yacht

Radar

VHF radio-telephone

Chart table
finger light

R D/F battery
portable

Electrical
panel

Echo sounder

Engine dials

digital presentation
of data from sensors

Chart stowage under

possibly in an "envelope," as they call those linen-backed chart folders, or a plastic cover and put under the mattress of the navigator's bunk.

Unless there is some ruthless weeding out, the chart table will be the crew's receptacle for their car keys, dark glasses, wallets, pop tapes, old sailing instructions, girlie magazines, spare batteries, sheath knives and various technical manuals. My first move on joining for a trip is to clear the chart table of everything of this nature into a bin liner and stow it in the heads.

Other designed stowages within easy reach of the chart table should be provided. Here I admit that we are moving on from the bare necessities to include many nav-aids commonly found in cruising or racing boats:

The electrical switchboard, with the navigation and mast-
head lights on separate switches, a switch to illuminate
the steering compass with an accompanying dimmer rheostat, the engine starting switch and a voltmeter to inter-
rogate the batteries before and during charging
Echo sounder display
Log-speed console and display
Wind direction and velocity displays
Any hyperbolic aid (Decca or Loran-C) or Sat-Nav
Radio telephone
A simple pocket calculator fixed to a bulkhead for dealing
with speed-time-distance problems
More sophisticated calculators, which can go all the way to
replacing every nautical table and solve celestial naviga-
tion problems, are best kept in the chart table drawer.
Ship's clock
Barometer
Spare compass unit
High-intensity flashlight and / or Aldis light for signaling.

Given the above the navigator can readily monitor the
yacht's progress. He should be situated so that it is simple to
get his head-and-shoulders into the hatch to take bearings or
verify any shore features by visual confirmation. He would be
well advised to have his own pocket flashlight and binoculars.

The cruise director

The navigator has more to do than seeing that the right charts
are on board and getting the boat from A to B. He should also
act as hotel manager to the skipper, especially in a boat carrying
more than four in the crew. The general plan of the voyage or
race should be displayed on a small sketch, explained to the
crew before departure and kept up-to-date. The plan will show
courses and distances on all legs of the voyage, the times of
HW and the duration of the ebb and flow of each tide.

Also displayed for the duration of the voyage is the watch
list and routine to be followed. Yachtsmen argue endlessly
about the best system to be employed. There's a lot to be said
for the Navy system of four-hour watches with split two-hour
dog-watches in the evenings (to avoid the same people doing
the Middle every night). A 1230 turnover at the end of the
forenoon watch ensures that lunch is not eaten too early. A
popular variation of that is to keep four-hour watches by day
and four three-hour ones at night. It depends on the weather,
the number of competent helmsmen in each watch and the
degree of concentration called for. In submarines we stood
watches on a straight two-on, four-off rotation. One advantage
claimed is that a maximum of three and one half hours in the
sack at any time keeps watchkeepers more alert and in the
tactical picture. Whichever system is adopted the navigator
should keep an eye on seeing that the watches are called, fed
and relieved on time. Nothing saps morale quicker than slop-
piness in this area. Washing-up, keeping the bilges low and
the batteries topped up should also be the subject of timely
reminders from the nav-station.

On a long voyage in easy conditions a three-watch system is
desirable, even if you only have a crew of three. Be ready to
go to two watches if the weather turns sour. Alternatively have
an extra offwatch hand on call, snoozing under cover in oilskins
and safety harness.

The navigator must catch the weather reports and handle
any compulsory race-reporting by R / T. There are views about
weather broadcasts, since their predictions are by no means
infallible. Too often they lead to unwise early or late sail
changes or holding too far off rhumb line in anticipation of a
wind shift. Rod Stephens never allowed his crews to listen to
weather forecasts for those reasons. My view is that the shipping forecasts should be respected before setting out on a
cruise or passage but, once at sea, it is best to keep an eye on

the barometer, the clouds and the behavior of the wind. The weather you have to deal with is here and now, not what some aspiring TV pundit has to say from the London Weather Center.

The weather actuals are often a better indication of what is to come than the area forecasts (see Chapter 8).

Also on display in the nav-station should be the complete sail inventory, with areas, cloth weights, limit of wind speeds, sheeting positions for each sail. Each sail bag and its normal stowage should be indicated by an abbreviated designation, as shown below:

Log books

It is perfectly possible to make local passages without the formality of recording them, but even when not racing, it is vital for the navigator to keep an accurate deck log if the voyage is out of sight of land, overnight or in poor visibility. In the Royal Navy and many merchantmen two logs are kept: a deck log, entered in pencil by the OOW or quartermaster, recording events as they happened; and a Fair Log, written in ink from the deck log and in due course forwarded to the Admiralty or the shipping line's head office.

A misdemeanor by an officer, short of meriting a court-martial, would be entered in the Fair Log in red ink and signed by the commanding officer at an uncomfortable ceremony at a table with a green baize cloth. "I had occasion this day to reprimand Lieutenant O'Hare for his negligent handling of HM Ship under my Command during close maneuvres on the screen." Meaning: Mick ordered the wheel to port on executing a Blue 18 turn and missed cutting Captain (D)'s ship in two by a coat of paint. This procedure was known as "logging." In a well-organized wardroom this page would then be used for lighting a cigar and a new one inserted before forwarding it to Their Lordships. Since they ended up unopened in a warehouse in North London, no harm was done.

In days gone by some merchant navy Fair Logs were taken

Bag No.	Color	Sail	Area	Weight	Max. Wind	Stowed	Sheeting
H 1	red band	Heavy No. 1 Genoa	900	11	18	forepeak stb aft	23 inboard
SP1	green	Max. spinnaker	1600	1.5	18	Nav bunk	Quarter blocks
TRI	white	Storm trisail	350	17	60	Pt fr'd cockpit	Boom end

very seriously indeed. One company used to require all chart-work to be plotted over courses marked up ashore beforehand in Indian ink. Every chart used during the voyage had to be forwarded to head office for scrutiny by the Marine Superintendent. These were compared with the Fair Logs to ensure that neither had been cooked and that the company's routing policy (10 miles off most headlands and always within two days' steaming of the nearest other ship of the same line) had been observed. Officers' promotions depended partly on not deviating from these guidelines. The company thus saved millions on insurance and salvage.

Happily no such standards are required of yacht navigators, but, apart from their nostalgic value, they are invaluable in the never-ending process of knowing where you are. Time and again it is necessary to reconstruct your plot. Without a reliable deck log you might as well be blindfold.

Like protractors and parallel rulers the best format is what you are used to. There are many log books available from chandleries. Most of them are too big or too inflexible for my taste.

I rely on the Imray Laurie Norris and Wilson Navigator's Log Book. It is a loose-leaf book between solid splashproof plastic covers: measuring 10½ in across by 7 in deep, so fits neatly into the standard bookshelf above. By unscrewing two brass bolts, extra pages can be added. Or, before a long trip, all the previously used pages can be taken out and stowed, out of harm's way.

Each page is ruled off with a narrow column on its left (for the time of each entry) a generous space for describing the relevant event and five more narrow columns on the right. None is designated. So start by doing so, adding extra column(s) as may be needed:

Time	Voyage from Cowes to Plymouth Remarks	Bar	Log	Tuesday, August 14, 1979 Co	Sp	Wind
0005	Down to 2 reefs, small staysail	990	37.9	315	8	SSW8
0040	JR out on boom to reeve off last reef	986	59.0	285	8	SSW9
0235	Fastnet bg 280	980	59.0	285	8	SSW9
0345	Tacked to port on parting jib sheet	980	65.1	280	8	W9
0504	Fastnet abm to port	980	73.5	190	9	W9
0636	*Marionette* lying a-hull. No assistance needed. Listened out on Ch.16. First inkling of scale of problem	982	86.2	135	9	WNW9
1045	Call cookie at 1130 50 miles from Rock av 8.9 kts	994	723.5	135	9	WNW8

Those are extracts from the log of the Swan "47" *Toscana*. The "JR" who walked along the boom to reeve off the third slab was none other than John Rousmaniere whose subsequent book *Fastnet—Force 10* is a classic.

Note:

(a) Times are local, as on ship's clock.

(b) Remarks are as they were written at the height of the storm.

(c) The normal practice of hourly or half-hourly entries was abandoned during the horrendous two-and-a-half-hour battle to get round the Rock against the new 30-ft WNW seas building over the old SSW swell.

(d) Barometer readings have been added as an extra column. The fall of 10 mbs in two and a half hours spelled real trouble—as if we needed telling.

(e) Only the last two digits of the log reading are entered.

(f) The course and speed entered are those which the helmsman reported having averaged since the previous entry. Note: courses ordered and steered are always to the nearest 5° magnetic, on the assumption that no one can sail an intermediate course with confidence. These are invaluable, not only in concentrating the helmsman's mind, but for manual plotting as a check against other aids (we were outside Loran-C cover, had no Decca or Sat-Nav).

(g) The winds entered are supposed to be their true direction and strength on the Beaufort Scale. Since then, I have decided to enter them as Magnetic and their velocity in knots, because that is how we read them off instruments and relate to the ordered course.

(h) In other circumstances, such as Gulf Stream sailing, an extra column is added to record seawater temperatures.

The left-hand facing page is blank. On this race I find much useful information has been added there. On the first page all legs of the race are listed, giving course and distances for each:

Leg	Co (T)	Dist (nm)
Start-Hurst Pt	252°	11
Needles-Anvil Pt	255°	19
Anvil Pt-Start Pt	259°	70
Start Pt-Lizard	264°	63
Lizard-Runnelstone	290°	18
Runnelstone-Longships	323°	5
Longships-Fastnet	310°	168
Fastnet-Bishop	136°	151
Bishop-Lizard	094°	48
Lizard-Rame	068°	46½
Total		599½

HW Dover BST	Sat 1406	Sun 0231
		1452
HW Devonport BST		Sun 0954
		2210

The last page of that log recorded the defects:

¾ oz spinnaker blown out
No. 4 Genoa boltrope ripped out
Top 3 main battens need replacing
After heads U/S
Stb bow light flooded
Man overboard light shorted out
1 jib sheet parted

And it summed up the end of the race:

Finished at 15 23.59 close astern of *Midnight Sun*, ahead of *Matrero* and *Alliance*. Secured Mill Bay Dock alongside *Uin-na-mara*.

Sailed 631 miles in 97 hrs 14 mins. Av 6.49 kts (6.15 kts on rhumb line)

Logged 665 miles; 5 percent over-log accounted by adverse balance of tides encountered.

The log of taking the boat over to English Harbor subsequently in a strictly cruise mode with three watches of two each makes different reading. The menu for each meal is recorded on the left-hand page, while a periodic muster of consumables is all recorded. Ten days out from Puerto Rico at the southern tip of Gran Canarias, we recorded the following (figures in brackets indicate consumption so far):

Vino blanco	9	(13)
Tinto	18	(14)
Vodka	2	(5)
Scotch	3	(1)
La Ina	3	($\frac{1}{2}$)
Rum	$2\frac{1}{2}$	(4)
Brandy	$1\frac{1}{2}$	($\frac{1}{2}$)
Port	$1\frac{1}{4}$	($\frac{3}{4}$)

"Discounting secret supplies"

Five days later we were down to 22 gallons of fuel, five bottles of vino, three-quarters of a bottle of "non-Gallic" cognac and one sherry, but hadn't hit the Scotch. The log recorded Devil's Island as the nearest point of land, 945 miles away. Concorde's double boom was noted on its way from Caracas to Paris. "Hands to bathe," each 1,000 miles from the

Canaries and distances left to run were logged. And so on until anchoring in Freeman's Bay, seventeen days two hours forty minutes out, having made good 7.05 kts for 2,895 miles at 169 miles per day.

It's all in the log book.

The ship's book

An invaluable addition to the navigator's bookshelf is a loose-leaf reference book containing all the data needed to operate the boat efficiently, especially those needed at short notice. It should include:

- Times and heights of HW at your nearest Standard Port. Any local tide tables.
- The sail inventory, stowages and sheeting positions.
- The compass deviation card.
- Photostat of latest IOR, IMS or other rating certificates.
- Photostat of ship's papers and docking plan.
- Speed / r.p.m. table under power.
- Dutchman's log table.
- Table of breakeven speeds while reaching off.
- Sources of weather forecasts: frequencies and telephone numbers.
- Safety equipment checklist, giving stowages and dates of last certification.
- Extracts or digests from all the technical manuals covering the boat's machinery and electronics.
- Crew roster, names, addresses and telephone numbers for homes and offices. Next-of-kin particulars.
- Useful addresses and telephone numbers: boat yard, designer, sail maker, yacht clubs, chart suppliers, taxis, restaurants, etc.

3 THE PLOT

Conventions and symbols on chart work

Times are expressed in four figures as shown on a twenty-four-hour clock. Thus 9 p.m. is 2100—not 2100 hours—just 2100. Sometimes a suffix may be added to indicate the Time Zone which the ship's clock is keeping. The 15° straddling the Greenwich meridian—that is, from 07°30W to 07°30E—is where Greenwich Mean Time rules. It carries the suffix "Z."

For each 15° band of longitude the clock lags one hour behind GMT to the west and keeps one hour ahead to the east. This ensures that the clock times of daylight are approximately the same on any given latitude. 07°30W to 22°30W is Zone +1 on GMT, while 22°30W to 37°30W is Zone +2, and so on. Strictly speaking and in any case where ambiguity might arise, for example, in timing a distress message, you should suffix the time with the number of hours slow or fast your ship's clock is on GMT. Thus the Eastern seaboard including the Bahamas is (+ 5), while Bermuda and the Caribbean from Puerto Rico to Trinidad are (+ 4). Where daylight saving time is in force these numbers are reduced to (+ 4) and (+3) respectively.

If you fly out to Hong Kong or even Long Island Sound to navigate a yacht, the first thing to do is make sure you know which Time Zone you are in. All celestial navigation tables and almanacs are based on GMT. Fortunately the WWV resolutely adheres to GMT, so you can pick up its time signal at least once an hour. All local time signals are listed in the almanacs. My tip is: keep a spare clock or wristwatch on GMT all the time. For practical purposes, when putting a position on the chart just use the four figures of ship's time.

Distances should always be expressed in nautical miles and decimal fractions. It is fortunate that there are 10 cables (each of 200 yds) in a nautical mile. Thus 4.3 nm is 4 miles 600yds. Do all your chart work and planning in nautical miles. Distances should be read off the vertical scale of latitudes at the side of the chart at or near the latitude you are in. All digital logs present their information in nautical miles and two places of decimals.

Depths and heights, including those of lighthouses, are still shown in feet on U.S. charts, but Canadian and European charts increasingly use meters to a single decimal place. Just remember that 1.8 meters, usually written as 1m8 or shown on a chart as 1$_8$, is 6 feet, or 1 fathom. U.S. charts show the height of a navigational light in feet, whereas the others give it in meters, using a small "m." In all cases its visibility range is given in nautical miles ("M"). Thus the same light shown on a U.S. chart as 49 ft 25 M would be 15 m 25 M on the others.

The characteristics of lights and how they are abbreviated have also undergone a change during the recent adoption of metric charts. The descriptions of coastal features are mostly self-evident, such as an estuary is now shown as "est" whereas formerly it was "esty." But the lights themselves need a mild degree of acclimatization. Here are the main ones:

Oc is a single occulting light, which means a light showing more light than dark.

Oc (2) shows two short dark breaks in each cycle.

Oc (2 + 1) is a composite group occulting light with two occulting sequences either side of a single flash in each period.

Iso shows equal light and dark periods.

Fl is a flashing light with less light than dark; not to be confused with F, which is a fixed light.

Fl(3) is a pattern of three flashes of light broken by longer periods of dark used to be shown as GpFl(3). In most cases the duration of each cycle is shown as "20s," meaning 20 seconds from start to finish of each cycle, sometimes shown as "20 secs." This is the key one to put your stopwatch on when making a positive identification of a new light just raised.

Q replaces the old QkFl for a light which flashes between 50 and 70 times per minute, so that it has the appearance of a rapid blinker. Even quicker flashers—80/159 times a minute—are VQ. And there is a rarely seen UQ, which is the Ultra Quick flashing light. IQ is an interrupted series of quick flashes—a sequence of fast flashes broken by no light. Another rare bird is the light that flashes its identity in a continuous repetition of a Morse letter. That is Mo(K) for a light which flashes -·- all the time. The colors of lights are self-evident. If not otherwise stated they are white lights. Sometimes they are mixed, when they may be AlWG, which means an alternating white and green light. A WG light is one showing white and green in different sectors at the same time.

Buoyage systems

Generations of North American sailors have been brought up on "Red Right Returning," their hallowed system, which is still in widespread use. This features Black buoys which may be unlit or carry Green or White lights on the port hand *when entering from seaward*. To starboard are Red buoys, which may show Red or White lights or be unlit Red nuns. Midchannel buoys are Black and White, while preferred channels are Red and Black (see p. 44).

Intracoastal Waterway Navigation Aids

The whole system is laid out as seen by a vessel entering from north and east, heading south and west.

On the port hand: Black buoys with ODD numbers, square Green daymarks and, where shown on the chart, lights of any characteristic.

On the starboard hand: Red buoys with EVEN numbers and red triangular daymarks. They may also be lit.

Midchannel buoys: Black-and-White vertical marking, which may be lettered and have octagonal Black-and-White daymarks. When lit they show a White light only.

Dual-purpose buoys marking a meeting of two channels: buoys on either side of the channel show, in addition to the port and starboard-hand system described above, a small Yellow square on each buoy and daymark and a Yellow triangle on each one to starboard.

Mississippi River System, Used on Western Rivers

To port as seen going upriver: Black buoys with White or Green flashing lights and square Green daymarks.

To starboard: Red buoys with Red or White flashing lights. There are triangular daymarks in Red and Pink.

Midchannel buoys: Preferred channel to starboard show Black over Red buoys, with Green over Red square daymarks and White or Green IQ lights. If the preferred channel is to port the buoys are painted Red over Black with triangular daymarks and Red or White GpFl(2) lights.

Uniform State Waterway Marking System

To be left to port: Black buoys with White ODD numbers and Green light or reflector.

To be left to starboard: Red buoys with EVEN White numbers and Red light or reflector.

There is a cardinal buoyage system, with Black-over-White buoys telling the vessel to pass to the east or north of the buoy, while Red-over-White indicates passing to the south or west. Additionally, Red-and-White candy-striped buoys indicate that a vessel must not pass between that buoy and the nearest

IALA BUOYAGE

Cardinal Marks

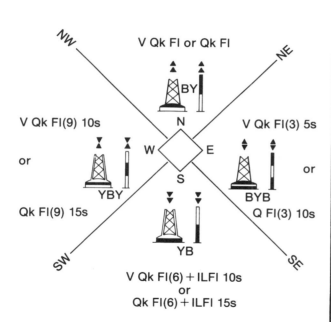

V Qk Fl or Qk Fl

BY
N

V Qk Fl(9) 10s
or
Qk Fl(9) 15s

YBY
W   E
S

V Qk Fl(3) 5s
or
Q Fl(3) 10s

BYB

YB

V Qk Fl(6) + ILFl 10s
or
Qk Fl(6) + ILFl 15s

Buoys indicate safe side of a danger
on which to pass

Lateral Marks

Can topmark

R

Lt R – any
rhythm

Direction
up-channel
from seaward

Cone topmark

G

Lt G – any
rhythm

to mark sides of navigable channels

Other Marks

2 B sph topmarks
Lt W Gp Fl (2)

BRB
ISOLATED DANGER
MARKS
safe water all round

R & W
SAFE WATER MARKS
Sph topmark
Lt W Iso, Occ or 1 LFl
ev 10s

Y   Lt Y
SPECIAL MARKS
not for navigation
X topmark

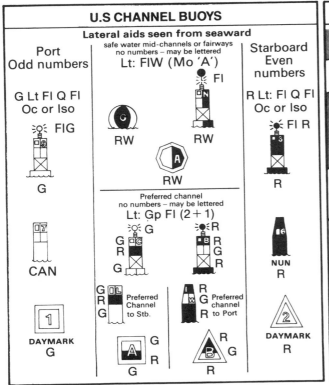

U.S CHANNEL BUOYS

Lateral aids seen from seaward

Port
Odd numbers

G Lt Fl Q Fl
Oc or Iso

FlG

G

CAN

DAYMARK
G

safe water mid-channels or fairways
no numbers – may be lettered
Lt: FlW (Mo 'A')

Fl

RW   RW

RW

Preferred channel
no numbers – may be lettered
Lt: Gp Fl (2 + 1)

G   R
G   R
G   R
G   R

G   Preferred
R   Channel
G   to Stb.

R   Preferred
R   channel
R   to Port

A   G
     R
     G

B   R
     G
     R

Starboard
Even
numbers

R Lt: Fl Q Fl
Oc or Iso

Fl R

R

NUN
R

DAYMARK
R

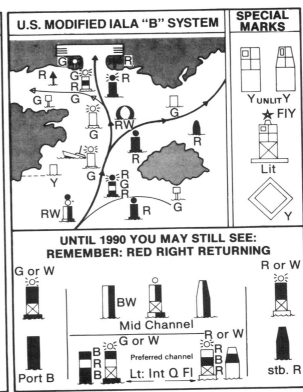

U.S. MODIFIED IALA "B" SYSTEM

SPECIAL MARKS

Y UNLIT Y

FlY

Lit

Y

UNTIL 1990 YOU MAY STILL SEE:
REMEMBER: RED RIGHT RETURNING

G or W

BW

Mid Channel

Port B

G or W

Preferred channel
Lt: Int Q Fl

R or W

R or W

stb. R

shore. Regulatory markers are usually White boards with Red trim and the message spelled out in Black (e.g., 5 m.p.h.).

IALA Buoyage System in North America

North America has a longer coastline than Europe and many thousands of inland waterways governed by different state and federal authorities, besides the U.S. Coast Guard. So it is not surprising that the United States has lagged behind the rest of the world in introducing the new IALA system. Instead the United States uses an interim one of its own which features green can buoys with odd numbers (!) and green lights to be left to port on the way upchannel, with red buoys and red lights to be left to starboard. These include truncated red conical buoys always referred to as "nuns," as opposed to their green opposite numbers known as "cans." Safe channels are red and white, while preferred channels (a sensible category rarely seen in Europe) are red and green.

IALA buoyage systems

The whole of NW Europe has now conformed with the lights and buoyage system (A) introduced by the International Association of Lighthouse Authorities (IALA) over the past decade. It embraces all the new chart notations mentioned above and elsewhere in this book. It is logical and consistent. The complaint most frequently heard is that the new green flashing lights on all conical starboard-hand buoys—that is, ones to be left to starboard on your way in from seaward—are not as easy to pick up as the old white flashers. Many have been intensified recently, but they remain a problem against the background of shore traffic signals and starboard bow lights in ships under way. Buoys and marks to be left to starboard have odd numbers, starting with number 1 at the outer end of the channel. The port-hand ones have even numbers.

It is important to remember that the cardinal marks (all Black and Yellow) tell you on which side it is safe to pass. There is logic about their topmarks and lights:

N-cardinal mark has two triangular topmarks pointing upward (i.e., toward the North Pole).

S-cardinal mark has its topmarks pointing downwards, toward the South Pole.

W-cardinal topmarks (apex-to-apex) make a letter "W" on its side, telling you that it is safe to pass to the west.

E-cardinal topmarks (base-to-base) from the Greek letter "E" signifies deep water is to the eastward.

Even their light characteristics are logical, going in clockwise order from:

N-cardinal—one quick flash
E-cardinal—QFl(3)
S-cardinal—QFl(6)
W-cardinal—QFl(9).

Courses and bearings are always expressed in three figures as degrees True. Thus 5° off True North is expressed as 005°. The old cardinal points are never used except in conversation, when they must be assumed to be Magnetic (e.g., SE is S45E, NW is N45W). But the habit of describing a "point" for about 10° (actually 11¼°) dies hard, for example in saying that a ship has been sighted two points on the port (or starboard) bow.

Elsewhere in this book I have urged navigators to **Think True**—that is, to convert all bearings and courses from Magnetic to True before plotting them. When in doubt, the suffix "T" or "M" should be added, but it is far easier to carry the approximate compass correction in one's mind and apply it at source. In most yachts this means just the Variation.

Arcs of lights are expressed in degrees True from seaward. Thus the white sector of a light may be shown as 030°–330°, which means that it flashes white 30° either side of North True when observed from seaward.

Plotting and fixing

The prime function of anyone responsible for navigating a boat is to maintain an accurate plot giving an updated EP at all times. The EP is the Estimated Position as opposed to the DR (dead reckoning). The EP takes account of tide, leeway and windage. Every position I mark on a chart has one of the following notations against its time and log reading:

Fix, meaning spot on, either by virtue of visual bearings a reliable Decca or Loran fix, or a celestial shot of three or more stars yielding a small cocked hat. Strictly speaking, the latter is an observed position (Obs-Pos) but "fix" is mostly used. It is the navigator's banker marked on the chart by a dot in a circle (⊙), which can be relied upon after the fog has set in. Sailing *Roundabout* back from Copenhagen after the One-Ton Cup in 1966 I left a guest artist on the tiller after clearing the roads off Copenhagen. Around 0500 I awoke to realize that we were hard aground and in thick fog. There had not been a single entry in the log or on the chart for four hours, so it was anyone's guess where we had fetched up. We backed off and sailed a reciprocal course until we picked up an identifiable navigational landmark, but it was a creepy feeling.

DR is the boat's dead reckoning position arrived at by simply plotting the course steered and the distance run according to the log. It is indicated by a cross (+).

EP is the boat's estimated position after allowing for all the known variables. Its accuracy depends on the navigator's input of the variables. It is a lot more reliable than the DR, which is what most yacht navigators tend to plot. The EP should be shown by a dot inside a triangle (△).

Nowadays most skippers think their electronic nav-aids do away with the need to keep a meticulous EP. All I can say to that proposition is that in the last twenty years of navigating yachts equipped with the most sophisticated nav-aids that money can buy (or the rules of racing permit) I have never yet completed a season without having to fall back on the EP plot. Ah-So (the Japanese computer-assisted read-out from Loran-C or Decca) sometimes chucks his hand in, with blinking amber or red lights telling the navigator he is on his own.

That is why so many boats on the Bermuda Race fail to hit off the NE Breakers buoy on the nose. Indeed, it is not unheard-of for million-dollar IOR boats to miss the island altogether.

If you aspire to be a Royal Navy submarine skipper you may be comforted by the thought that SINS (Submarine Inertial Navigation System, a complex three-dimensional system of highly accurate gyros monitoring the deviation from True North) is designed to give your position at all times accurately enough to hit Colonel Qaddafi's sauna bath at a range of 2,500 miles. But the hard-nosed Perisher Teacher in charge of the qualifying course makes it his business to find out how you get along without SINS. He gives each pupil a twelve-hour spell dived in Inchmarnock Water in the confined approaches to the Clyde without access to any nav-aids other than the compass, the rev-knot table and the echo sounder. The periscope is manned by a safety officer whose job is to prevent the blind-folded "skipper" from driving the submarine up the main street of Lamlash on the island of Arran.

The skill of the navigator in plotting his EP is of paramount importance. It even ranks ahead of his local knowledge in identifying a headland like the Dodman or Anvil Point in a fleeting break of the visibility. Unhappily most yacht navigators do not know the difference between EP and DR.

Going offshore, the most important moment is to be able to lock the plot onto a reliable departure fix. Ideally this should be a tight set of three bearings on visual shore features. But a carefully taken bearing on a dipping light is better than nothing, using the light's stated range as accurate to ± 1 mile at the moment when it drops down to being just a loom on the horizon. The precise cutoff moment can be determined by standing up in the cockpit and seeing the full light, while sitting down it is only a loom. Obviously this only applies in good visibility.

In making an EP plot it is necessary to lay off all the factors which will cause the boat to deviate from her ordered course. Much has been written about velocity triangles, but it is really very simple: plot the course and distance planned over a given time, then lay off the resultant of all the factors which will push the boat off that track, join them up and read off the course and speed made good (see p. 51). How to allow for leeway is a matter of judgment and experience of the boat. In a powerboat it is not a factor to be reckoned with. To judge the leeway being made by a sailboat, a rough indication can be found by looking over the transom at the wake. If it grows out to weather by 5° or more it is a clear warning that the boat is sliding to leeward by that amount while on the wind. Running or broad-reaching the leeway is negligible, but the navigator's problem is to know how much to lay off when the course is on the wind.

Here I must disagree with some of the pundits, who recommend allowing 2–3° leeway while on the wind, depending on its strength. But the fact is that the harder it blows the more the helmsman tends to luff up, thus making his own correction for leeway. However, a boat with a shallow canoe body like *Perseverance*'s 27 in will slide off to leeward at an alarming rate, even with her centerboard down. The practical figure for her was not less than 10° leeway.

A powerboat with a high profile will be susceptible to leeway in a beam wind, but it is probably within the accuracy of the helmsman's course made good.

Plotting in Practice

Starting from your departure from any well-known feature such as Montauk Point Light, St. David's Head or the Rebecca Shoals Light, lay off the ordered course in degrees True, with the ship's time and log reading alongside its beginning: 0925 (22.7) means the fix was taken at 0925, when the log read 22.7. I always put the log reading in brackets so as to avoid any confusion with the time. Always assume you are about to run into impenetrable fog.

At 1000 it is time to settle into the routine of reading the log and marking up the EP on the chart. It now shows the log reading 25.9, in which case your DR position has advanced 3.2 miles along the plotted course. So measure 3.2 miles off the latitude scale and mark the new point on the course with 1000 (25.9).

If at the same time you get a reliable fix by shore bearings which puts you elsewhere, mark the chart 1000 (25.9)FIX. The discrepancy may be due to log error or tidal effect, but it is your most up-to-date certain position and should immediately be accorded the respect of a datum.

Never rub out chart work until you are quite sure you have no further use for it. You may want to check back to clear up some doubts, for example to find out when or where the log (or more likely one of the electronic robots) started giving false readings.

A fix is not something you get from a pusher in Greenwich Village just after midnight, but is just as morale-boosting, without being addictive. It means any position for your boat

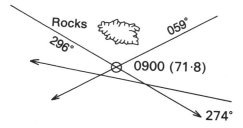

on the chart that can be relied on with certainty. Using a hand-bearing compass this will involve taking three or more bearings at least 30° apart from each other. Once they have been converted to True bearings and laid off on the chart, with luck they'll cut in on top of each other, in which case you have a fix, thus:

0900 (71.8) FIX

But if the plotted bearings do not fall so obligingly, you end up with a "cocked hat." If the area enclosed is small, take its midpoint as your fix. If however it is large, you should treat it with caution and always assume your position to be on the edge of the cocked hat nearest any off-lying danger: It could be the moment to take another set of bearings.

The most reliable visual bearing of all is a range, obtained

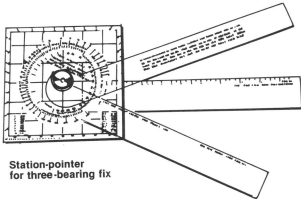

**Station-pointer
for three-bearing fix**

by bringing two identifiable and charted shore features into line with one another. A classic one in daily use is that marking the Cleveland Ledge channel, the approach to the Cape Cod Canal. The QKFlG light at the SW extremity of the breakwater is brought into line with a FG on shore on course 015°. A transit is always designated as $\emptyset$ on a chart. Its great beauty is that the slightest deviation from it, whether due to cross tides or bad steering, is immediately apparent.

Experienced navigators accumulate a wealth of private transits, especially for racing around the buoys. The starting line at Cowes sometimes has its outer limit mark 2.5 miles away, with one's view of the determining transit on the Royal Yacht Squadron battlements blotted out by hundreds of competitors' sails just when you most need to know whether it is safe to go for it. The trick is to get right on the line long before it is cluttered up by other boats and, from the pulpit right for'ard, select a transit high up on the island shore which will be visible above the press of sails. It may be the right-hand edge (→|) of

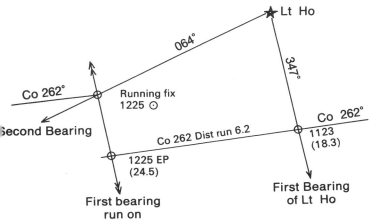

Plotting a running fix

the Gloster Court flats in line with an oak tree on the skyline in Northwood Park.

Do not use fairway buoys for transits, as they tend to shift position slightly with the ebb and flow of the tide. Temporary buoys, such as inflatables laid by the race committee, can safely be assumed never to be in their advertised position. Starts from committee boats also call for private transits.

A transit coupled with a vertical sextant angle of the seaward mark forming it constitutes a fix of high reliability.

A running fix, much loved by instructors who make them look good on a blackboard, depends for its accuracy on knowing your precise course and distance over the ground between each bearing. But it may be better than nothing when only a single shore mark is in sight (e.g., the Nantucket Light Tower when passing a long way to seaward or in poor visibility). The navigators take two consecutive bearings of the light at intervals giving no less than 30° change of bearing. After the first bearing has been laid off, the plot is run on to the point where the second one is taken. Then the first bearing is transferred forward by the distance run since it was taken. A parallel bearing line is drawn. Where it cuts the second bearing is the position of the running fix.

The accuracy of this method is totally dependent on the EP. In strong tides it can be considerably in error.

Horizontal sextant-angle or station-pointer fix measures the lateral angle between each of three prominent landmarks. By use of a special station-pointer with three adjustable arms you can then determine your exact position. Without a station-pointer you can reach the same result by drawing out the three bearings on tracing paper and then slew it around until you set the only point where it fits all three shore marks. I reckon it to be rather an academic ploy and too fiddling for practical purposes in a small boat.

Another trick is to make use of the fact that a right-angled

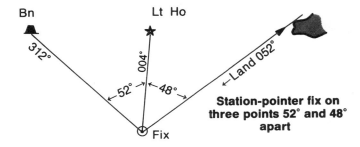

Station-pointer fix on three points 52° and 48° apart

isosceles triangle has the two sides enclosing its right angle of identical length. So, take a bearing and note the time and log when a landmark is precisely 45° on the bow. The distance made over the ground until it comes abeam will also be the exact distance at which you are passing the mark to seaward.

A useful approximation for judging the distance by which you are going to pass outside a mark is to note its relative bearing, measured clockwise or anticlockwise from right ahead at a time when you have a reliable range, for example on raising a light. Provided you maintain course, the distance off when you get there will be:

$$\frac{\text{relative bearing in degrees}}{60} \times \text{the range}$$

Thus a light first spotted 24 miles off when 5° on the starboard bow will be left 2 miles when passing abeam. The sum is

$$\frac{\text{rel.bg } 5°}{60} \times 24$$

This mental aid holds good for relative bearings from right ahead to about 55° on the bow. It can also be used for judging the distance off track an oncoming ship will pass, assuming you are not closing on a collision course. Take the angle on the bow at which you observe the oncoming ship, divide it by 60 and multiply by the range for the amount of clear water there should be between you at your closest point . . . all things being equal.

Range (or distance off) can be obtained by measuring the vertical angle of an object of known height. For this you can either use a sextant or an approximation based on finger widths or the proportion of the field of view filled in your binoculars. Once you have the angle and the height, a useful mental aid for rangefinding is:

$$R \text{ (range in yards)} = \frac{H \text{ (height of object in feet)}}{A \text{ (vertical angle in minutes)}} \times 1150$$

It follows that whenever the height observed in feet is the same as the angle it subtends in minutes the range is 1,150

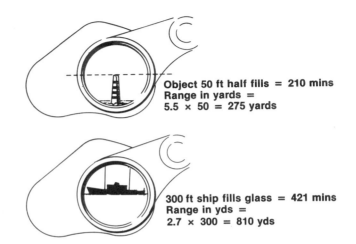

Object 50 ft half fills = 210 mins
Range in yards =
5.5 × 50 = 275 yards

300 ft ship fills glass = 421 mins
Range in yds =
2.7 × 300 = 810 yds

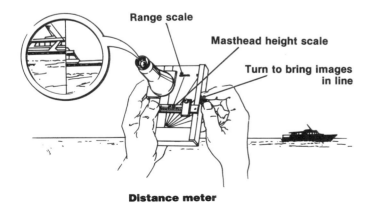

Range scale

Masthead height scale

Turn to bring images in line

Distance meter

yds. Thus a 100-ft light measured at 1°40 is 1,150-yds distant, while a 200-ft tower at the same vertical angle is 2,300 yds away (1.15 nm), and so on.

Since the field of view of a pair of 7 × 50 binoculars subtends a fraction over 7° (421′),

when the object fills the field of view   R = 2.7 × H
if it half fills the field   R = 5.5 × H
if it occupies a quarter of the field   R = 11 × H

for simplicity, round it off to 3H, 6H and 11H, and you won't be far out.

There are special tables in the almanacs to give you the answer with greater accuracy, especially when using a sextant (see p. 89).

49

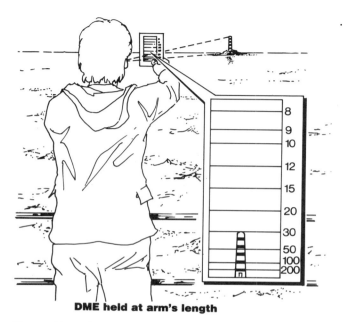
DME held at arm's length

Distance Measuring Equipment (DME)
This is a card with a graduated frame cut in it. When held at arm's length an object of known height can be read off against a scale which in turn will give its range off an accompanying graph. There are other variations of this same principle on the market, but this one is obtainable from Wansbrough-White & Co, c/o Neil Simpson, Marinaid, 445 Roxton Road, Toronto M6G 3RS, Canada.

Visual nav-aids There is nothing more reliable than a positively identified shore feature, whether it is a lighthouse, a church spire or an edge of land. But never ignore other

sightings on which some reliance can be placed. The track of a ferry or a merchantman following the recommended course in a separation zone can be useful, as are the guard ships on offshore distance races. If you get them right ahead or astern their course will be correct within 5°. The other certainty is to take a bearing when you are precisely abeam of them (the moment when the front of the bridge superstructure disappears) and then add or subtract 90°.

Commercial aircraft on flights from New York to Bermuda can also be useful. Sailing across the Atlantic on the tradewind route I found it comforting to have the boom boom of the Concorde signaling its approach en route from Caracas to Dakar.

Other nav-aids Even if you have a constant latitude-longitude readout from Decca, Loran-C or Sat-Nav, don't count on any of them. In the 1983 Fastnet I navigated Arthur Emil's beautiful 51-ft Petersen-designed *Artemis*. She was equipped with every known hi-tech nav-aid. Running down from the Fastnet to the Scillies we found ourselves in thick fog. With the wind from the WNW the foghorn on the Bishop Rock was inaudible until we were almost on top of it. If we had relied on any of our electronic nav-aids we should certainly have driven onto the rocks not far from where Sir Cloudsley Shovell met his end.

On that occasion our EP was based on a fix obtained by the echo sounder picking up the Labadie Bank cutting in with a good D/F bearing on Round Island on the north side of the Scillies. The tidal effect was negligible, so we hit off our desired landfall one mile south of the Bishop with no problem.

Later I patented an audio-nav tape which was intended to talk skippers into unfamiliar ports. An old submarine friend of mine, Peter Lucy, devised the circuitry necessary for the tape to be switched on and off at appropriate times, like 150 yards short of each mark upon which a new course had to be shaped. This depended on an input giving course and speed over the ground with some accuracy. After two years' hawking the idea around the various manufacturers of electronic nav-aids we had to accept the fact that no one could produce the required degree of accuracy at a price which yachtsmen would be prepared to pay—if at all.

Radio direction-finding (D/F) also needs to be used with caution (see p. 65).

Tidal currents Only the Swiss, the PLO and Aztecs sail in waters without any tidal effect. So the strength and direction of the current must be built into any EP. The popular idea that the ebb and flood tides cancel each other out in any twelve-hour period is a comforting notion, but not one that works in practice. For one thing it depends on your speed of advance (SOA), which might be 4 kts at the start of the passage, slowly building to 7 kts. The wisest move is to lay off your planned course on the chart, marking off where you hope to be each hour. Then take the aggregate tidal effect and run it off from the end of your plot as though you had sailed the boat in that direction. A line joining the start point and the end of the tidal offset will be what you should actually achieve.

Most tidal atlases give the strength of the tide at Springs and Neaps, so you must interpolate according to the state of the moon or the range of the tide. Whether reading off from the tidal information table on a chart or from a special tidal atlas the net result should be the same. Thus the mid-Channel ebb at Neaps might read as follows:

HW Dover	1 hr after	250°	0.5
	2 hrs after	250°	1.0
	3 hrs after	245°	1.5
	4 hrs after	245°	1.5
	5 hrs after	250°	1.0
	6 hrs after	250°	0.5

By inspection the total tidal effect over six hours is 6 nm 248°. Assuming our own speed through the water at 5.5 kts on course 175° we now plot 33 nm on 175° then transpose it 248° 6 nm, giving course and speed made good 183° for 35 nm (5.83 kts).

Or, in the example below covering only 1 hr 15 mins, the log recorded 7 nm run on course 103°. The tidal information from the chart or a tidal atlas shows that the current will have set 3.6 nm in the direction 155°. This is plotted after allowing 3° leeway to show course and speed made good over the ground of 118°—8 kts.

When your boat speed is not consistently on 5.5 kts, for example in a flat spot, the sums have to be reworked. This is one of the navigator's preoccupations when trying to lay off a course to hit a buoy like CH 1, where the tide runs strongly across the lay line.

In developing a plot of your voyage it is necessary to mark the EP against the log reading and time on the chart once an hour, on top of any intervening fixes which might present themselves. The latter may be passing close to an identifiable buoy or crossing a transit (two shore features falling into line) at a known distance offshore. This can be determined by cross

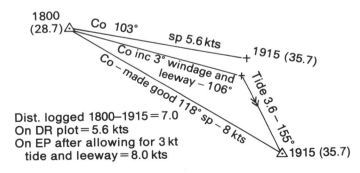

Plotting an EP

bearings or by measuring the height of the nearest object with a sextant. The Royal Navy used to have small monocular station keepers which gave the range in cables (200 yds) of an object of known height by bringing the reflected image down to the bottom of the directly observed view of the object. I picked up my last one for £2, complete with polished mahogany case. They are now available in crummy plywood boxes for £650. A sextant does the same job, but is a bit clumsy to wield. Nautical almanacs all include tables for converting the observed sextant altitude for a known height into a distance. While racing, this is the best method of determining whether you are gaining or losing on a competitor during a downwind leg (see p. 49).

The OPC is a constant source of anxiety to the navigator. It stands for "other people's chart work" and can include such gems perpetrated by the watch on deck as the longitude scale having been used for laying off distances, ignoring the decimal point on a digital log presentation or plotting a magnetic course without allowing for Deviation or Variation.

The correct scale for measuring distances on a Mercator projection (which includes nearly all charts in common use) is from the latitude appropriate to the waters in which you are sailing. Thus, to lay off 5.6 nm on the plot, open the dividers to that distance as shown on the vertical side of the chart opposite the latitude you are on at the time.

A common source of egg on the navigator's face emerges when he transfers a plot from one chart to the other without the benefit of a recent fix. On a long offshore voyage always check back to see that the distance plotted bears close relation to your assumed SOA. It is surprisingly easy to gain or lose ten miles in the process.

Log errors At the end of a passage always compare your recorded log distance with that which you have actually sailed over the ground, especially on long reaching or running courses.

If the comparison doesn't hold good after applying the net tidal effect, you may be tempted to adjust the log. Usually this is done in percentage terms by a clicker screw in the back of the console, but first check with the maker's manual (it should be in your Ship's Book). With a towed log you vary the pitch of the vanes according to a scale provided. My experience has been that one tends to overreact on suspected log errors. If you believe that the log is underreading by 10 percent, try an adjustment of 5 percent. Most logs are very accurate, provided they have been installed or streamed in accordance with the maker's instructions.

Compass errors The likelihood that the master steering compass will develop a significant error during a voyage is hardly worth considering. To be on the safe side, check the sun's azimuth (i.e., true bearing) on rising or setting (see p. 7). The greatest source of course error can be attributable to the helmsman's simply not knowing what course he has averaged when called for a log entry. This often happens while racing, when a skillful light-weather helmsman may well sail on the boat-speed presentation, without even noticing what course he is steering.

Going for speed downwind

On a downwind leg even while cruising it pays to reach off, thus increasing apparent wind speed and boat speed. Sherman Hoyt taught Tom Sopwith a painful lesson on this subject by broad-reaching around *Endeavour* on a dead downwind leg when the Brits were heading for a 3–0 lead in the 1934 challenge for the America's Cup.

Controversy between the cockpit and the nav-station often surrounds the amount which can be profitably steered off the rhumb-line course. The figures are interesting and not generally understood. They are shown graphically on the opposite page:

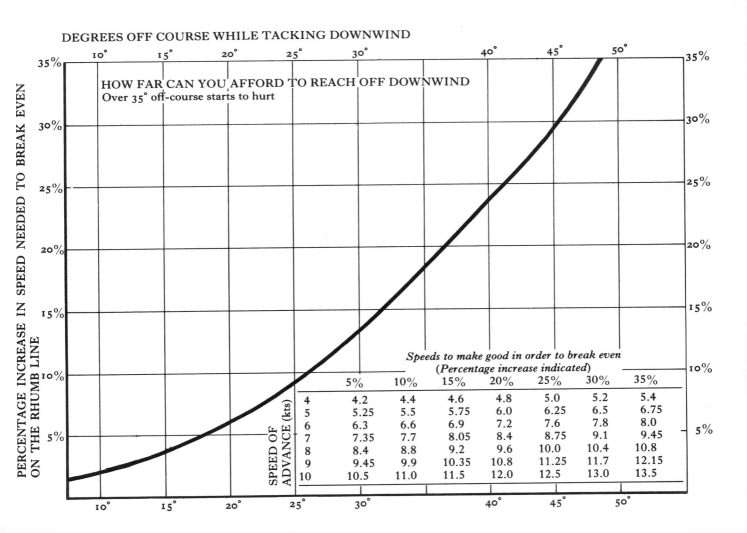

DEGREES OFF COURSE WHILE TACKING DOWNWIND

HOW FAR CAN YOU AFFORD TO REACH OFF DOWNWIND
Over 35° off-course starts to hurt

PERCENTAGE INCREASE IN SPEED NEEDED TO BREAK EVEN ON THE RHUMB LINE

Speeds to make good in order to break even
(Percentage increase indicated)

SPEED OF ADVANCE (kts)	5%	10%	15%	20%	25%	30%	35%
4	4.2	4.4	4.6	4.8	5.0	5.2	5.4
5	5.25	5.5	5.75	6.0	6.25	6.5	6.75
6	6.3	6.6	6.9	7.2	7.6	7.8	8.0
7	7.35	7.7	8.05	8.4	8.75	9.1	9.45
8	8.4	8.8	9.2	9.6	10.0	10.4	10.8
9	9.45	9.9	10.35	10.8	11.25	11.7	12.15
10	10.5	11.0	11.5	12.0	12.5	13.0	13.5

Up to 25° off course you only need to find another 10 percent of boat speed to be gaining ground toward your objective against a boat which stays on the rhumb line.

At 30° off it becomes 15 percent, so that boat speed has to go up from 6 kts to 7 kts to pay off. Thereafter it gets increasingly unattractive.

Forty degrees off is 23 percent below rhumb-line speed, so that you have to get 7½ kts to keep pace with a 6 kt boat on the rhumb line.

At 50° off you need to find 36 percent speed increase, or 8¼ kts to hold your original 6 kt SOA.

As the course deviation increases into left or right field you need to bear in mind how far you are getting away from your objective.

Navigating high-performance offshore powerboats

In a high-performance powerboat making over 40 knots offshore there is always the worry that the compass will not settle, with each slam into a head sea spinning it like a roulette wheel. So I devised a sun compass, lifting the idea from the Long Range Desert Group's jeeps in World War II. This was no more than a sundial set forward of the driver's windshield with an azimuth ring adjusted for the anticipated time of our being halfway across Lyme Bar with 20 miles to go to the Skerries buoy south of the entrance to the River Dart. It worked beautifully.

Navigating a fast-powerboat offshore, especially racing, calls for a technique of its own. Any idea that you can use a chart, dividers or a protractor is farcical. My solution was to have a tabulated flight plan giving the courses and distances between each mark on the course. These were presented as hours, minutes and seconds elapsed at every speed liable to be used during the race, accompanied by special descriptions of the lead-in features ashore: high rise apartment building at Boscombe, TV masts at Slapton, the right-hand edge of the trees near Christchurch when running in from the sou'west to pick up the North Channel buoy, and so on. Below are some extracts from the 1970 flight plan.

The same waterproofed card gave the extra speeds necessary to break even with our SOA if it was necessary to deviate from the straight course in order to get easier riding conditions on the long run across Lyme Bay. This idea first came to me when

Stage	Dist nm	Speed in knots						
		25	27½	30	32½	35	37½	40
		Times in hrs and mins						
Start–Sconce buoy	25.8	1.02	57	51½	48	44	41½	39
N Channel–Branksome	13.0	31	28½	26	24	22½	21	19½
Portland–Skerries	44.4	1.47	1.37	1.28	1.22	1.16	1.11	1.06½
Torquay–Portland	41.0	1.38½	1.29½	1.22	1.16½	1.10	1.05½	1.00½
Portland–N Channel	35.4	1.25	1.15	1.11	1.05	1.01	56½	53
N Channel–Finish	12.5	30	27½	25	22	21½	20	18½

I was taking a Bertram 38 from Newhaven to Cowes. It was thick fog, visibility about 50 yards. Running with two turbo-charged Caterpillar diesels there was no chance of hearing a foghorn. So I timed a run from Newhaven to a point 2 miles downwind of the Owers lightship. When the stopwatch said we had run off the distance, I cut the motors. It was magic: there was the fog signal booming its head off right in front of us. Next thing we nearly hit the lightship. This technique also has its application to sailboats motoring in fog without the benefit of radar or any other form of reliable electronic nav-aid.

The higher your speed under power the more prudent it is to stop and take stock of any doubtful situation before proceeding. Last summer I was a guest in a 16 kt powerboat heading for Cherbourg with less than total confidence in the compass. The visibility was less than a mile when a lighthouse suddenly appeared out of the spray and rain. Its light was not on, and it was too quickly identified as Cap de la Hague. Instead of killing the motor and getting a D/F check, we cheerfully headed east through what later turned out to be hazardous waters strewn with rocks. It soon became apparent that we had altered on sighting Cap Levi and had to retrace our steps gingerly to the westward.

Fog

Another situation which calls for more than straightforward DR plotting is finding one's way around in thick fog without the benefit of radar or reliable hyperbolic aids. Then the navigator soon reveals whether he possesses the two qualities sought by Napoleon in selecting a marshal—he's not only got to be good; he's got to be lucky as well.

He has available to him only those nav-aids which are unaffected by zero-visibility conditions. More than ever it is necessary to know precisely what credence to place on the log, compass and echo sounder. The latter can play a key role if the topography of the seabed has distinctive features, such as when crossing a clearly defined depth contour. In certain circumstances it can add to your peace of mind if you stay in depths which would put a supertanker hard aground.

A big tanker or container ship making 18 knots will keep on going straight ahead for nearly a mile before her ship's head starts to respond to an emergency wheel order. She will come to rest up to 3 miles after Full Astern has been rung down. Even if the bridge watchkeepers spot you on their radar and she has sea room in which to maneuver, there is no certainty that she will miss. In confined waters a new version of the right-of-way between sail and steam is enforced by local bylaws requiring yachts to keep clear at all times. My advice is to observe that rule even in a chance encounter in mid-Atlantic. The autopilot does not keep a lookout. Some call it the Gross Tonnage Rule.

Such thoughts were uppermost in my mind soon after clearing the breakwater at Dunkerque in thick fog while delivering *Crusade* to Cowes. We were embarked along the narrow buoyed channel between the sandbanks and the French coast when thick fog descended. We felt our way buoy-hopping to the seaward end of the fairway and then were faced with beating across the main shipping lanes to reach the English coast, like crossing Broadway in rush hour blindfolded. Heavy sirens boomed all round. No two members of the crew agreed about their bearings, as is often the case in fog. So we made for Cap Gris Nez 30 miles away, staying inside the 5-fathom line, going about the moment the echo sounder said we could be sailing in waters with ships drawing 30 feet. That limited our liability to being run down by a trawler or a ferry. One of them passed close enough ahead for her wash to slop into our cockpit, but we didn't get a glimpse of her. Happily the fog lifted soon afterward and we resumed our rhumb-line course.

The range at which radar will detect an echo is governed by

the height of its antenna and the height of the target. It is near enough line-of-sight propagation. If you want to go bananas in a hurry, invest in a radar intercept receiver, which will pick up a transmission while it is too weak to make the return journey to its own antenna. These are much favored by motorists with two strikes against them for speeding, always assuming they are on the same frequency as the police radar trap.

Their use at sea is limited by the fact that there are several radar frequencies in use, whereas commercial intercept gear will probably be limited to one of them. Even so, in crowded waters you'll be constantly on Red Alert.

Even in less frequented waters, the art of feeling one's way from one buoy to the next can go sadly awry if your chart shows only the major buoys. This is often the case with U.S. and Canadian charts. Making our way to St. Peters at the entrance to the Bras d'Or lakes we pressed on in thick fog in order to make a rendezvous in the locks. Confronted with having to negotiate the last few miles around the rocks in the Grand Grieve, our chart showed no buoys or beacons, so gave no indication whether to go round them clockwise, or the other way. We guessed wrong and found ourselves hard aground short of Jerome Point. The other channel was well marked but only on a large-scale chart, which we did not carry.

Fog Signals—Fewer and Quieter
Most lighthouse authorities recognize that improved nav-aids and complaints from environmentalists point the way to cutting back on the number and audibility of fog signals.

Many production boats are delivered with the steering compass as the only nav-aid installed. Within months some proud owners have equipped them with every known aid to navigation from radar to autosteering—and then leave their boats alongside a marina for over 300 days a year.

At the outset, you alone can decide what you need beyond the Bare Necessities of Chapter 1. This in turn will depend on where and how you plan to sail—and what you are prepared to spend. If your ambition does not extend beyond local cruising in coastal waters, there is little point in going for Sat-Nav. Likewise radar need not be considered if your boat is too small to carry the antenna or scanner (typically 25-in dia weighing 24 lb, but in some sets up to 3-ft dia and 40-lb weight) securely mounted at a reasonable height above the water, preferably not less than 12 ft. Or you may be going for flat-out racing and do not want the penalty of windage or weight aloft. Loran-C is not for you if you are going to be outside its expanding coverage (see p. 60). Decca still covers most of the Atlantic coast of Europe and the British Isles but will soon be replaced by Loran-C.

The RORC's 1985 decision to lift all restrictions on hyperbolic and transmitting electronic aids has coincided with a proliferation of makes and types of equipment on the market. Clearly it is not sensible to rely solely on a salesman offering only his own products. Whereas most chandleries stock a fair selection of nav-aids and probably have all the brochures, few of them have staff who are qualified to give you all the pros and cons.

So ask around for a firm or a consultant who deals in all makes of equipment and can install whatever you choose. Major yachting centers have this facility available, and many have demonstration sets close at hand. You pay no more than list price and can negotiate a fixed cost for installation, knowing that it will be done expertly, avoiding such pitfalls as electronic or magnetic interference with other sets. For a new boat there are people who will design the whole nav-station around the instruments of your choice.

With unit costs coming down and the large number of new instruments continually becoming available— each offering new and more sophisticated solutions—it is worth getting what you need. Some of the maxi IOR flyers add $100,000 to their price before the navigator feels he is properly supported and the crew has sight of enough repeaters.

Radar or Loran-C?

With Loran-C or Sat-Nav around $1,700 without repeaters, many owners will have to start by deciding which one they can afford. The table of comparisons on page 58 between typical yacht radars and position fixing systems may help:

For the weekend cruising yachtsman forced to make a choice there is no doubt that the advantage lies heavily with radar. The navigator's problem is limited to bringing the boat within radar range of his intended landfall. It is important that the antenna be properly mounted. This is a big proviso, pretty well excluding all sailing boats under 25 ft unless they are ketch or yawl rigged and have a mizzen mast for mounting the scanner.

There is a portable hand-held radar which plugs into the ship's 12-V system or operates from its own battery. It is usually worn on a sling around the neck of someone on the foredeck. The antenna is incorporated and fixed, so bearing sense is obtained by swinging the set to pick up the echo on a

Characteristics	Radar	Position-finding device (Decca or Loran-C)
What the navigator sees	Continuous trace of coastline and all ships and other targets in range	No visual plan display No data other than own ship
Presentation	Cathode ray tube with own ship in center and concentric ranging rings on $\frac{1}{2}$–8-m scales Ship's head marker with relative bearings of all targets	Digital readout of lat-long and hyperbolic lines on special lattice charts Digital readout of course and speed being steered, or made good between fixes including speed-time-distance and all vector problems
Practical accuracy	$\pm$ 1° bearing $\pm$ 15° vertical beam width $\pm$ 50-yds range (strobing error)	$\pm$ 0.1 miles (200 yds) in summer, often better $\pm$ 0.2 miles in winter Affected by proximity to land (e.g., in estuaries) and some propagation anomalies
Bad weather	Sea clutter masking small targets out to 1 m. Heavy rain has local blanketing effect	Unaffected
Range	Approx line-of-sight subject to power output. Radar horizons = $1.22 \times \sqrt{\text{Antenna + target heights (ft)}}$ e.g., Antenna 16 ft should pick up 60-ft Lt Ho at $10\frac{1}{2}$ nm	Within 250 nm of master station for Decca, 1,000 nm for Loran-C

Weight and Sizes:
  Antenna
  Display/console
	
	25–40 lb 25–30-in dia
	20–25 lb 10 in sq or up to 15-in deep
		
		$1\frac{1}{4}$ lb 3-ft whip
		$2\frac{1}{2}$ lb 10-in x 5-in x $2\frac{1}{2}$-in deep

Power (12 V)	6.5 amps	0.2 amps
Watch out for:	Siting scanner within 4 ft of compass; people with heart pacemakers are at risk	Vulnerability of antenna to rigging or sails

All systems offer continuous solutions so long as power does not fall below acceptable limits.

narrow horizontal beam, in the manner of radio D/F. Its practical use is confined to picking up buoys fitted with radar reflectors at a range of 1½–2 miles, depending on the sea state. In the 1985 Halifax–St. John Race there was visibility of less than a cable all the way from the start to the finish 240 miles away, but the Whistler, as we called it, managed to pick up the critical buoys which were turning marks off Cape Sable. We stormed over the finish line under spinnaker without even seeing the committee boat, but they had us on their radar and, once again, the Whistler obliged. Commercially the set is now known as "Ranger Radar."

Radar Beacons (Racon) Certain lighthouses and buoys are fitted with transponders which pick up an extraneous radar transmission and fire it back so that it appears as a rectangular slug on the transmitting ship's PPI display. In some cases it may have a coded identification (e.g., the Seven Stones LV, which the *Torrey Canyon* failed to notice, emits a letter "O"— at the tail end of its trace). Racon beacons are designated "Racon" on Admiralty charts. Their particulars can be found in any nautical almanac.

Depending on antenna height, Racon beacons should be picked up at 10 miles.

Radar reflectors The echo returned by a small fiberglass boat is unremarkable and easily lost in rough seas. To enhance the echo in poor visibility you should hoist a radar reflector as high as you conveniently can. There are two types:

(a) A diamond-shaped structure made of three flat interlocking aluminum sheets between 12″ and 20″ square. The advantage claimed for this type is that it can be dismantled and stowed away flat in a canvas pouch. But strong men have been driven to drink when it comes to reassembling it and getting all its corners securely locked into a rigid structure. Experience of putting together oriental wooden puzzles helps.

(b) A GRP cylinder about 2-ft long and with a 9-in diameter, filled with aluminum foil, has a nominal echoing area of 9 sq ft, which is a substantial improvement on the biscuit-tin model described above. They look neater and can be more easily secured so as not to flap around while hoisted, but at about $120 they cost three to four times more than the diamond puzzle does.

An even better solution would be a 3-cm waveband transponder which amplifies the signal from the detecting radar and throws it back with interest. At one time it was proposed that the RORC should make these available for yachts racing across the steamship lanes in the English Channel, but it was decided that 150 beefed-up lozenges all painted simultaneously on the radar receiver of a merchantman would create too much confusion.

Or perhaps sparmakers will oblige by building radar echo enhancers into the rig.

Sat-Nav
Existing satellite navigation receivers in yachts rely on the U.S. Navy's Transit system, six satellites which have been in polar orbit since 1964 and are no longer evenly spaced. There are certain limitations:

(a) An initial DR accurate to ± 60 nm has to be fed in, and then a warm-up period of fifteen minutes is necessary. The receiver digests the signals from the satellite during each pass lasting about fifteen minutes. It measures the doppler shift (high frequency on approach, low going away), notes its closest point of approach and is automatically told enough by the satellite's message to work out an instant fix for the boat.

(b) Satellites passing below 20° or over 70° latitude are unreliable and will be rejected by the receiver.

(c) The interval between fixes is one to one and a half

hours, depending on one's own latitude. If one or more satellites has an off day, the fixing interval can stretch to over four hours.

(d) A computer updates the latitude-longitude position between fixes but is susceptible to errors of input, especially of speed made good over the ground. The practical accuracy for a stationary boat is ± 400 yds (0.2 nm) provided all goes well. Each knot of error in own speed input will induce 0.2-nm error.

The advantages for Sat-Nav are:

(a) It is the best available alternative to Decca or Loran-C outside their coverage area, especially if astro-nav is not available.

(b) The antenna is small (12 in × 7 in), nonrotating and weighs just over 2 lb. It can be located anywhere above decks.

(c) Its power consumption is low, using 12–36 volts at 20 W. Some sets have an internal battery, giving fifteen minutes' backup life in the event of a ship's power failure.

The Transit system will be in service at least until 1994.

Decca

This British hyperbolic navigation aid gives continuous fixing within its area of coverage—up to 250 miles off the Atlantic coast from the North Cape to the SE coast of Spain. All being well it will deliver its claimed accuracy of 200 yards at 100 nm. Latitude and longitude are shown by digital presentation. It needs a verifying departure fix to get its act together quickly. It can coach the helmsman to preset latitude-longitude positions known as way-points.

Loran-C

The well-proven long-range aid to navigation (Loran-C) covers within 1,000 nm of the coast of the United States, the Mediterranean from the eastern coast of Spain to Cyprus and the waters of the British Isles and Norway to the north and west of a line joining the Fastnet Rock and the Skaggerak. Its position accuracy is generally ± 0.3 nm but has its lapses in certain areas of poor propagation. It operates on 100 kHz and measures the time difference (TD) between signals from a master station arriving at two or more slave stations. These are plotted on special lattice charts giving the hyperbolic lines of TDs in microseconds. Coverage is gradually being extended to the whole of the British Isles and its approaches, when it will replace Decca for yachts.

All modern sets translate this data to latitude-longitude digital displays, *but:*

Always do an occasional check of the latitude-longitude displayed on the receiver against a plotted fix of TDs on a Loran-C chart, because it may sometimes be more accurate than the microprocessor solution. Another reason for not relying solely on the latitude-longitude display is that there may be times when one set of TDs is out of kilter and showing amber or even red warning lights on the receiver, while the other is still reliable.

In 1985 I was navigating *Toscana* from St. John, New Brunswick, to Mount Desert Island near Bar Harbor, Maine, normally an easy trip of 125 miles along one of the most beautiful coastlines in the world. But the visibility was less than a cable, the wind was 20 knots on the nose and I had a flight to catch. Soon after sailing, our Loran-C receiver served notice that it was no longer prepared to help.

Our progress motor-sailing through the narrow rockbound straits between Grand Manan Island and the Canadian border had to be hand-plotted from one whistle buoy to the next. We often had to cut the engine to pick up the sound of the next buoy, then creep up to it for positive identification.

Ten miles short of Mount Desert we broke out into sunshine and maximum visibility. My sleepless night could have been made less anxious if I had spotted soon enough that one of the Loran-C TD-lines ran straight through the Grand Manan Straits to our destination and that it had performed faultlessly, although its "pair" was unable to produce any kind of a latitude-longitude fix.

However, Mount Desert Island is shown in *Eldridge's Pilot Book* as an area in which Loran-C is liable to local propagation errors of up to 1,300 yards, so you can't win them all. Some modern sets eliminate these anomalies for you.

Loran-C is to all intents and purposes as accurate as Decca in its own waters. American microchip and computer technology has led the way with dozens of different makes of receivers, each neater, simpler to operate and sometimes cheaper than last year's model. It always needs a whip antenna of its own, generally fitted to the taffrail.

The global positioning system (GPS)

GPS has seven satellites in orbit already, mostly in military use, but only providing about six-hours' coverage a day, although U.S. manufacturers selling the system to yachtsmen interfaced with (i.e., linked to) Loran claim "up to eighteen hours" in the northern hemisphere. The full GPS system, giving twenty-four-hour worldwide instant fixes, will require eighteen satellites up there, plus three spares parked in orbit, all designed to be launched from the cargo bay of a space shuttle. Hence the delay of GPS coming into service, now admitted to be 1991 or later.

It does not work on doppler measurement but on timing the difference between several satellites' transmissions and their reception on board. For civilian users including yachtsmen its accuracy will be ± 100 yards, deliberately degraded to prevent hostile nations' enjoying the ± 15 yards planned for the military. It looks as though the sets initially will cost as much

as a half-tonner, but no doubt the Japanese will have other ideas.

Omega

Until GPS becomes a reality and within reach of a weekend yachtsman's budget, there is only one worldwide continuously available position-fixing system. Here I discount celestial navigation, for it is surprising how far you can sail without seeing the sun or getting stars under conditions suitable for hacking them down.

In 1960 I was dismasted in the Transatlantic Race in *Drumbeat*. We made it to St. John's, Newfoundland, where her old spare wooden mast duly arrived on a Bowater newsprint ship from London. The subsequent crossing to Brixham took a little under eleven days. We sailed through the iceberg belt in thick fog and then ran before a succession of warm fronts the whole way over, without ever seeing the sun or the stars. Our landfall was verified by echo sounder and radio D/F bearings on Round Island, at the northern end of the Scillies.

The system which might have helped under such circumstances is Omega, developed by the U.S. Navy around the same time the U.S. Coast Guard was perfecting Loran-C. It has worldwide accuracy of ± 2 nm by day, but possibly twice as much by night. It transmits on VLF (10–14 Kc, or kHz nowadays) not far off the frequencies used to communicate with submerged submarines. The master stations all require antennas of up to 2 miles in length, usually slung between adjacent mountain peaks, as they are in Norway, Alaska, the Rockies, Australia, Japan, Argentina, Liberia and Reunion Island.

Unlike submarines, yachts can receive these signals on a whip antenna only 7-ft long, digested in a box no bigger than a Loran-C or Decca console.

Various propagation anomalies have to be allowed for and

special U.S. lattice charts used for plotting. However, all these difficulties can be overcome by having a differential Omega receiver which takes in rebroadcast laundered position lines accurate to within ¼ mile when you happen to be within 50 miles of one of the monitoring stations. Unhappily these are far between; for example, from Dover to Gibraltar is 1,250 miles, but the monitoring rebroadcast stations along the route (Cap Gris Nez opposite Dover, Ushant, Cap Finisterre at the NW tip of Spain and Lagos just east of Cap St Vincent) only cover 350 miles of the route. A modern receiver will come up with latitude-longitude.

For around $8,000 you can get a Tracor so-called global navigation system, which links Omega to Sat-Nav and keeps a continuously updated position on display.

On balance, Omega does not rate high on the weekend navigator's shopping list.

Integrated systems

(Only rich owners of cruising boats need read this section, or those who are liable to be invited to race in an IOR boat and want some understanding of the cross talk between helmsman, navigator and sail trimmers.)

Long before the RORC allowed computer-aided systems to take the inputs from any sensors (e.g., wind direction and speed from the masthead, speed and distance run from an underwater log, course from a transmitting magnetic compass and depth from an echo sounder) and display a wide option of tactical solutions, Brookes & Gatehouse offered its first Hercules system. This was accompanied by a list of functions which were on offer and a warning of those forbidden during RORC races. Some, such as calculating True Wind Speed and Direction or Vmg (the speed made good along the rhumb line), could be simply arrived at by manual plotting, using elementary velocity triangles. Meanwhile Hercules was doing it all for

you, at the touch of a button, but the navigator was not supposed to peek unless the boat was flying its ensign, and thus not under the rules of racing.

Brookes & Gatehouse was mainly using analog displays (clock-face) but, along with its evergrowing range of competitors, increasingly now offers alternative digital displays. Currently its super-Hercules 390 system for a raceboat will cost over $8,000 plus installation charges. Nowadays there are no restrictions against using the whole system during races.

Many of the functions on offer seem to be there more to demonstrate the versatility of the system than to answer any long-felt need. True enough, single-handed sailors can gain comfort from having alarm hooters sound off on any major change in wind direction or depth, but they have not prevented some spectacular shipwrecks, simply because, like commuters, sailors can sleep through alarm calls. Perhaps that may explain the disappearance of some single-handed sailors.

Battery voltage, seawater temperature, heel angle and timing an egg to boil can now all be shown on digital displays simply by selecting the right channel.

Many instrument makers recognize that the wide spectrum of information shown simultaneously to the helmsman can be confusing even to the most experienced racing crews and amounts to an expensive overkill for a cruising boat—like fitting a 747 instrument panel in a Tiger Moth. So now simplified sailing monitors are available, which confine themselves to presenting the log, speed, wind and battery voltage displays. One such is the B & G Hornet.

It is as well to bear in mind the following factors which can distort the end product of microprocessors and give the helmsman false guidance, mostly in very light winds:

(a) Even in a boat with a moderate mast height there will be days when the wind speed and direction may be different on deck to those at the masthead whence your sensors are sending down their messages to the instruments over the chart table. Some modern maxis have extra wind sensors fitted halfway up the mast, seeking to measure the average strength and direction of the wind which is powering the sail plan, rather than that which shows on the burgee or ensign.

As a schoolboy I recall being alone in a 9 ft 6 in Lymington Scow totally becalmed in the middle of the Solent when the entire J-Class fleet sailed through me at 6 kts, propelled by a breeze which only existed 75 ft above the surface. The bearded man at the wheel of *Britannia* had a familiar look and an unforgettable vocabulary, as he suggested I should get my bloody boat out of the xxxx way. American sailors refer to this phenomenon as "wind sheer." It has little relevance to cruising boats, most of which would have their kedges down or their motors on before the situation arises.

(b) Although carefully balanced and machined, there is some mechanical friction in masthead wind sensors, which can lead to erroneous inputs down below. There is also the effect of heavy rolling or lurching. These are especially apparent when the wind is from astern and the relative wind on the knife edge of zero.

Nowadays it is hard to find someone who is available to light a cigarette and let the smoke tell where the zephyrs are coming from. I recommend a Chinese joss stick on a wire stick which can be stuck on the cabin top and give off a steady slow-burning smoke signal. After all, the captain of a big aircraft carrier relies more on a smoke trace emitted along the flight deck near the axis of the catapult than from any instrument.

Some boat owners collect nav-aids like motorists do club car-badges, so I end this section with a word of advice to anyone putting total reliance in his instruments, if only because they cost him so much. Don't react too quickly to any change in circumstance or sailing efficiency being shown on the dials.

Don't rush into changing sheet settings; let them settle for a minute or more before deciding that the new data has to be acted upon.

On the last Bermuda Race I coined a phrase for our trigger-happy helmsmen and sail trimmers: DDD (digital dial dementia). The same people who are quite accustomed to applying the five-minute rule and making sure of the new breeze before initiating a sail change react as though they are ducking a mugger's knife when polar boat speed—an esoteric efficiency measurement drawn up for an individual boat on different points of sailing—drops a tenth of a knot.

Recently I heard of a freak error induced by blind obedience to Decca. A Class I ocean racer was leading the fleet, broad reaching on starboard on a black stormy night. When the skipper came on deck he noticed that the boat was now reaching off on the opposite tack, still making close to hull speed. "That was a big wind shift," he commented.

Not so. The helmsman was steering by a digital compass dictated by Decca guiding them to the next way point—an arbitrarily chosen tactical milestone, often the next mark on the course. He assumed they had overstood, and the black box was putting him right; or perhaps he thought they'd reached one way point and were now on course to the next. Somehow he'd missed the buzzer which alerts the navigator to the end of one leg and the start of another.

A lat-long check on the chart showed that the boat had sailed nearly a reciprocal course for 3 miles, which ultimately cost them the race.

The reason was that someone had inadvertently hit the man-overboard button on the set, which was now faithfully conning the boat back to the exact position where the nonevent had occurred.

It could just as easily happen with a Loran-C linked integrated system.

Radio direction-finding (D/F)

Radio and Radar Chart Symbols

All charts nowadays have a violet circle around the lighthouse or buoy carrying radio or radar aids. The letters alongside identify their functions, as follows:

Ro Bn	Radio beacon
RC	Circular (nondirectional) radio beacon.
RD	Directional radio beacon with the direction of its transmitting beam shown by a bearing over a pecked line. Thus 221° indicates a radio range on the bearing.
RW	Rotating loop radio beacon
Ro DF,RDF or RG	Radio direction-finding station
R Sta	Station offering QTG service
Aero RBn or RC	Aero Aeronautical radio beacon
Racon	Radar responder beacon
Ramark	Radar beacon transmitting without being triggered off by a ship's radar.

Omni-directional marine radio beacons operating on long-wave frequencies between 275 and 325 kHz have been used by yachts for over fifty years. The more powerful transmitters can usually be relied on to give a single bearing to an accuracy of ± 5° out to a range of 50 miles by day. The reliable range for getting good bearings by night is not more than 25 rm. The commonest form of receiver is one with a ferrite rod aerial mounted across the axis of a hand-held magnetic compass. Once the station has been identified by frequency and call sign (see nautical almanacs for this information) the D/F set is held as far away from the boat's magnetic influences as practicable, with the operator wearing a headset, rather than relying on loudspeakers against competing ambient noise. Most prefer a battery-operated set with no trailing power leads. Around $250 will buy one with push-button tuning and a trigger lock to clamp the compass rose and read off the null without losing it on the next lurch of the boat.

The station might be Brenton Reef Tower, off Newport, RI. It is listed and shown on charts as:

Call sign (signal)	"BR" — ··· ·—·
Frequency	295 kHz
Range	10 nm
Sequence	continuous

The majority of U.S. radio beacons transmit continuously, but some frequencies are shared by other nearby stations, each transmitting for one minute and every sixth minute thereafter. The order in which they are in sequence is shown by Roman numerals. Thus 306 kHz is used by Clinton Harbor, Connecticut (I), Little Gull Island, New York (II), Horton Point, New York (III), Clinton Harbor again (IV), Watch Hill, Rhode Island (V), and Horton Point, New York (VI). Each transmission lasts exactly 60 seconds, starting with the call sign repeated for 50 seconds and ending with a steady note for the last 10 seconds.

Having switched on and tuned to the precise frequency, be ready to use any one of various switching positions intended to filter out extraneous noise by use of the beat frequency oscillator (BFO).

To take the bearing during the 25-second steady note, hold the antenna as nearly horizontal as possible and sweep it gently back and forth across the point where the null occurs. This is the moment when the transmitted signal drops to its lowest point, or even cuts out altogether. The more distinct the contrast between the null and the D/F signal and the smaller the arc through which it is observed, the more reliable the bearing thus obtained. In practice it is better to note the bearing to the left where the audio note starts to diminish, than read off its right-hand edge, when it comes on strongly again. Split the difference and you have your observed D/F bearing. The wider the null arc, the greater the likelihood of error.

There are however a few sleepers in this neat-sounding procedure. The first is the quadrantal error induced by the radio waves being bounced or reflected off the boat's rig and structure. They have the effect of bending the signal. They are at their most pronounced in a boat with metal frames, rigging and guardwires which have not been "insulated" by having rope seizing at each end; the worst errors occur on either bow or quarter. Some D/F suppliers offer to swing the set against observed visual bearings of a D/F transmitter and fudge a "deviation" card which looks good—as any smoothed-out sinusoidal curve should—but in practice is not much help, especially since most D/F bearings at sea are taken when the boat is heeled over.

Reaching in toward the end of the 1984 Bermuda Race I picked up Gibb's Hill and Kinley Field D/F stations loud and clear with a small, well-defined null. There was no question of getting a cut from them, as the bearings were less than 20° apart. But both confirmed a suspicion that there was an easterly set which had carried us too far off our desired rhumb line for a racing landfall. Loran-C had been of dubious value since we had pounded our way through wind-against-current for several hundred miles and the whole set was in intensive care, with silicone spray trying to dry off the antenna junction box.

We were about to tack to the westward, when a single sun sight at right angles to our track showed that both our precise D/F bearings had been slewed 15° by quadrantal error.

Some of the 1985 Admiral's Cup boats were still using a remote D/F antenna mounted on a staff above the taffrail with a morse cable drive to rotate it. Heeling error is reduced by tilting the antenna housing by hand into approximately the horizontal plane.

D/F bearings are also affected when taken at a narrow angle to a high coastline.

In spite of its drawbacks, radio D/F can be useful in rounding a headland on which its transmitter is sited.

Aero beacons have the advantage of transmitting continuously, but many are situated some distance inland with high ground intervening and introducing further errors.

Any kind of D/F bearing lends itself to being misread as a reciprocal bearing; but, except for transmitters situated in the open sea, such as Gibb's Hill, Bermuda, or Dry Tortugas off the Florida keys, the bearing "sense" is generally self-evident, but keep it in mind.

Calibration By prior notice to the lighthouse authority (Trinity House in Great Britain), you can arrange to get a transmission for calibration purposes within 5 miles of a few selected Ro Bn stations. They are listed in the almanacs, but I can't see the point in the rather formal procedure involved, when you can always pick up a shore station while on passage and check against visual bearings.

Details of Radio Aids The principal nautical almanacs and the *Admiralty List of Radio Signals*, Volume 2 contain all the information you need.

Other Radio Aids If you have a VHF receiver there are two additional radio aids which give a bearing accurate to ± 2° unaffected by any of the yacht's own errors in taking D/F bearings out to 30 miles in good conditions.

(a) *VHF Direction-Finding Service* operated by twenty coast guard shore stations around the U.K., each of which is shown on the chart with the symbol "RG." On a passage along the south coast they are located at Pendennis at the entrance to Falmouth, Rame Head SW of Plymouth Sound, Berry Head at the western end of Torbay, Portland Bill, Stenbury Head near

Ventnor in the Isle of Wight, Fairlight near Hastings and South Foreland, the most prominent white cliff of Dover. Lovers of the rollicking sea shanty "Spanish Ladies" will now know where Fairlight is, mentioned in the Grand Fleet's progress up-channel as the last headland before Dungeness. The full list can be found in nautical almanacs or the *Admiralty List of Radio Signals*, Volume 2.

This is a service for use in emergencies, but not necessarily terminal ones. For example a boat lost near a lee shore in bad visibility without radar or radio D/F functioning could follow the drill.

Constant watch ashore is kept on Channel 16, the universal distress frequency (156.800 MHz). If it is not a distress message the yacht should call on Channel 67 (156.375 MHz, the universal Coast Guard net). The shore station will call on the same frequency, giving the yacht's True bearing *from* the shore station.

There are also RG facilities on Guernsey at the airport 2¾ miles WSW of St. Peter Port and Jersey near La Corbière Lt Ho at the SW extremity of the island. Both listen on Channel 16 and Guernsey has Channel 67 for its working frequency, but Jersey uses Channel 82 (161.735 MHz).

If asked, certain Coast Guard stations will put out a signal for the yacht to check its own D/F bearings. The service is known as QTG and its transmitter shown on the charts with the letter R.

Consol Known as Consolan in the United States, this is a wartime long-range passive radio aid, calling for no more than an MF receiver, a Consol chart (or tables giving bearing lines) and an ability to count up to sixty and determine when the dots stop and the dashes start. In practice there is usually a blurred null which is middled to get the bearing. Thus 32 dashes and 21 dots, leaves 7 unidentified. The answer is 35½ dashes, 24½ dots.

The range is certainly up to 1,000 miles, so it calls for the application of half-convergency tables to allow for the difference between Mercator and Great Circle plotting. It is unsuitable for coastal navigation or for making a landfall. Furthermore the system is now obsolescent and reduced to one transmitting station in Europe: Stavanger on 319 kHz.

Forget it.

Navtex This is a simple telex receiver operating on a fixed MF frequency of 518 kHz using 12 V DC which receives a printout of urgent navigation notices to mariners, gale warnings, twice daily shipping forecasts, search and rescue (SAR) alerts, nav-aid alerts when any of the position-finding systems develop problems. It is compact, about the size of *Reed's Almanac*, can be left on "stand-by" using only a 2 ma trickle of juice, going up to 2 amps while printing incoming messages. A standard wire antenna is supplied with the basic set at about $800; a whip antenna for optimum reception will add another $150. Using the service is free.

The International Maritime Organization is aiming for all ships to carry Navtex, with the intention that one day there will be worldwide coverage within 200 miles of any coastline.

At present there are transmitters at Niton on the Isle of Wight, Brest-le Conquet opposite Ushant and Ostend, between them covering the whole of the English Channel comfortably, with others in Scotland and the Baltic.

The information put out is geared to the needs of commercial shipping and is not too comprehensive on coastal or inshore data. However, it is said that a small ships' service may be started up. Until it does, it is low on any yachtsman's optional extras.

Needless to say the Japanese have entered the lists, offering a receiver printing out not only Navtex but weather facsimile synoptic charts. (FAX).

Twenty years ago R/T was about as likely to be found in a weekend yachtsman's boat as in the family automobile. But, like household appliances, TV sets and music audio systems, they have ridden the microchip revolution in a buyer's market.

Since the advent of citizen's band radio (CB) and cellular circuits, you don't have to be head of Mogul Oil to keep in constant touch with the outside world. One enthusiast told me he had purchased a car telephone to avoid the frustration of pulling in at a pay phone and finding it out of order.

So it is with yachts. VHF radio-telephones are available for under $300. Within the limitations of their range (somewhat better than line-of-sight) and the number of channels with which they are equipped, they are very much on the increase. In North American waters there are very few boats other than racing dinghies or Hobiecats, which venture outside the breakwater without VHF R/T. It is mandatory for most coastal or offshore races.

Apart from calling in from seaward to book a berth or to alert the coast guard or customs, R/T is as important for your own safety as it may be for others in distress. A fire at sea or sudden flooding may give you time to get off a distress call by voice, in the certain knowledge that the coast guard and all commercial ships will be keeping a loudspeaker watch on the distress frequency, Channel 16 (156.800 MHz), even if you are out of range of a shore station. It is also useful for getting weather forecasts from the coast guard. Channel 6 (156.3 MHz) is reserved for ship-to-ship traffic.

Modern sets are light, compact, easily installed and no more difficult to operate than a TV set, unless you are tongue-tied or have not grasped the procedure (see p. 68). During the 1979 Fastnet Race only the 57 boats competing for the Admirals Cup had to carry VHF sets and had to report their positions regularly. The other 250 boats were required to carry only a signal light and distress flares for communicating with the outside world.

When the extent of the disaster which had struck the fleet became apparent, the BBC Radio News tacked on a message from the Race Committee asking that all yachts able to do so should report their positions. I switched on the VHF set, got an encouraging red light to show that it was powered up and identified ourselves to the outside world, with the ammeter flickering back and forth as I spoke. By this time there was a fleet of rescue craft and aircraft all talking on Channel 16, but no one answered. After repeatedly sending out an unacknowledged message, the skipper agreed to use his single sideband (SSB) HF transmitter, which had 8 times the power of the 25W VHF set, an independent antenna and a range of several thousand miles. It also cost five times as much.

Generally it is permitted to be used at only half power during some races and not at all in others, except in an emergency. On this occasion we got straight through via Portishead. Later we noticed that our masthead VHF whip antenna had been blown away in the storm.

Regulations to be observed

Compared to the complex licensing rules in the United Kingdom, there are few problems confronting a first-time owner of an R/T set in the United States. He does not even require an operator's license, but will soon be jumped on by the Federal Communications Commission (FCC) monitors if he breaks the rules or uses incorrect procedures. The FCC headquarters is in Gettysburg, Pennsylvania, and it is the government agency with authority over all radio and TV traffic. It will issue a station license for a short-range VHF set and, with it, the call sign for the boat. Any dealer will make the necessary arrangements and, at the same time, show evidence that the set is type-approved by the FCC. The maximum permitted output is 25 watts.

A longer-range single sideband (SSB) set with voice propagation up to 3,000 miles needs a permit from the FCC. One will not be issued unless the intended user already owns a VHF set.

Rules governing operating sets:
  (a) Follow correct voice procedures (see below)
  (b) Absolute priority to be given to distress traffic
  (c) Do not transmit on top of another station
  (d) Respect confidentiality of intercepted traffic
  (e) No obscenity
  (f) Do not use distress channels for routine traffic, although Channel 16 can be used for calling up another ship, if you then switch to another assigned channel. Recently an owner was fined $1,000 for having Channel 16 switched to "transmit" for seven hours, due to a defect in the set. It could have been $10,000 and a suspension
  (g) All transmitted messages must identify the yacht concerned
  (h) Ship-to-ship R/T transmissions in harbor are forbidden, but ship-shore is permitted.

Procedures

(a) First, make sure the channel selected is clear and then proceed, first naming the station being called and then giving your own identification. There are special calling frequencies listed for all shore stations. Do not call them on Channel 16. Now proceed: "Key West Radio (this is) yacht *Lulubelle*—

over." "Over" means you have switched off your transmitter and are listening for a reply. If you do not get an answer it pays to add "Do you read me?" which may bring in another station that can relay your message. When you have established contact, give your message clearly, where necessary repeating or even spelling phonetically words likely to be misread:

"Intend proceeding to join yacht *Nephele* . . . I spell, November Echo Papa Hotel Echo Lima Echo . . . at Cay Biscayne marina berth C for Charlie Two at 1615 . . . over."

The receiving station will give either "Roger" or "Received" and, if he has nothing further to add, "out," denoting end of conversation. If the message has not been received or understood, he should ask, "Say again," or "Say again after Cay Biscayne . . . over."

If in doubt, have the phonetic alphabet from Alfa to Zulu showing near your set with the phonetic numerals from Won to Zero.

(b) *Distress and emergencies on Channel 16;* VHF or 2182 kHz.

At any time of grave danger, go straight on the air with "Mayday" three times, followed by "This is *Lulubelle*" three times. Then add, "Mayday *Lulubelle* in position [bearing and distance from a fixed mark]" or, simply, "close to Buzzards Tower, am sinking . . . over."

An urgent message calling for immediate aid should be prefixed "Pan Pan Pan," then "All stations [three times] . . . this is *Lulubelle* in position . . . medical assistance for crewman unconscious with multiple injuries . . . over."

Unless safety of life is involved, the coast guard prefers to work on Channel 22. In the vicinity of a local rescue involving several ships, Channel 6 is recognized.

Urgent messages affecting all ships in a given area (e.g., a wreck, unlit buoy, suspected mine adrift) will be prefixed "Securité" pronounced *say-cure-it-ay.* Such messages are usually but not necessarily originated by shore stations.

(c) Ship-to-shore personal calls. The VHF channels manned and geared up to handle public correspondence traffic at the various ports around the coast are all listed in the almanacs. They are generally confined to the following channels: 24, 25, 26, 27, 28, 84, 85, 86 and 87.

Establish contact with the marine operator, identify yourself and, when answered, ask for a linked call to (area code) and number. Then settle how payment is going to be effected.

Channels 9, 69, 71 and 78 are for ship-to-shore use by pleasure craft, usually to a marina.

(d) Ship-to-ship calls. Calls from a private phone ashore to a ship can be made by contacting the high seas operator, tollfree on 1-800-SEACALL.

(e) Keeping in touch. Whenever you intend going further afield than your local cruising ground, it is wise to fill in a USCG Float Plan. This is a detailed questionnaire calling for full particulars about your boat, its equipment, crew and projected voyage. Once lodged it can save the rescue organization a lot of uncertainty should you be reported overdue or in some other difficulty. The form can be obtained from any coast guard station and most marinas. A call to the coast guard will get a blank form mailed to you. All the instructions for handling it are spelled out.

U.S. Coast Guard Search and Rescue Organization (SAR)

The USCG has prime responsibility for all SAR operations. They are directed from two centers:

The Atlantic Area Operations Center on Governor's Island, New York; telephone: (212) 668-7936.

The Pacific Area Operations Center is at San Francisco; telephone: (415) 437-3700.

For administrative purposes the Coast Guard is divided into districts, as follows:

First District (Maine to Delaware, including New York) is run from Boston; telephone is (617) 223-3644.

Fifth District (Maryland to North Carolina) is run from Portsmouth, Virginia; telephone is (804) 483-8527.

Seventh District (South Carolina to the mouth of the Mississippi, including all Florida and the U.S. Caribbean territories) is directed from Miami; telephone is (305) 350-5611.

Eighth District (Gulf of Mexico from the Mississippi to the Rio Grande) is run from New Orleans; telephone is (504) 589-6198.

Eleventh District (Southern California to Mexico) is run from Long Beach; telephone is (213) 499-5380.

Thirteenth District (Northern California to Washington) is directed from Seattle; telephone is (206) 442-5886.

The Maritime Provinces of Canada are controlled from Halifax, Nova Scotia; telephone is 426-2412.

Coast Guard stations are situated so that a ship in coastal waters should always be in VHF range on voice using Channel 16 (156.8 MHz). They also monitor 2182 kHz on MF, suitable for boats with SSB, and Channel 9 for C.B. distress calls. Channel 22A (157.1 MHz) is an alternate USCG distress frequency.

All stations, with their frequencies and operating data are listed in the different volumes of *U.S. Coast Pilot. Eldridge* and *Reed's* almanacs give details for the Eastern seaboard, but for the West Coast you should refer to volume 7 of the *Coast Pilot*.

FINALLY, NEVER USE CHANNEL 16 OR 2182 kHz FOR TEST TRANSMISSIONS.

6 AUTOMATIC STEERING

In a cruising yacht there is much to be said for having an autopilot controlling the tiller or wheel to keep the boat on a steady preset course or at a given apparent wind angle. Under most conditions "George" will do a better job than a helmsman, who can thus be freed to take shelter under the dodger, go below to put on a fix, make a hot drink or attend to an adjustment in the sail plan without having to worry about an involuntary gybe or being taken aback.

In a well-balanced boat with a reasonably long keel it has always been possible to take a turn around the tiller with the bitter end of the jib sheet and let the boat sail herself for long periods.

Running sufficiently far off the wind, which is to say when it is blowing from within 30° either side of dead astern, a very simple self-steering rig can be improvised as soon as you switch to a double headsail rig set wing-and-wing. Never mind if you don't have two headstays; the second jib can be set flying, then drop the main. Alternatively it might be possible to reef the main to approximately the same area as the winged-out headsail and regard the main boom as a second spinnaker pole, but it will need lazy guys to avoid coming up all-standing on a shroud. Thereafter follow the advice given in Colin Mudie and Patrick Ellam's hilarious book *Sopranino*, the account of how they showed the world that offshore distance races in boats under 20 ft LOA were perfectly possible. That led to the Junior Offshore Group and such events as the Mini Transat, the race from U.K. to Antigua in boats under 6 m LOA (21 ft).

Here's how they rigged up their self-steering gear for sailing in the Trade Winds, once making a day's run of 134 miles in the process.

Instead of having foreguys led to the eyes of the boat and each separately secured, they had an endless foreguy from the outboard end of one boom through a swivel block at the stemhead and back to the outboard end of the other boom. For adjusting this part of the rig, the guy was not secured there, but led back through a snatch block to a cleat on or near the mast. The after guys from each boom were then led through blocks and secured to the tiller.

Thus when the wind exerted more pressure on the leeward headsail, causing the boat to luff up, the weather after guy would be hauling the tiller up to weather, thus pushing the ship's head offwind until the while system was in equilibrium once more.

They had separate tiller lines rove off athwartships to limit the travel of the tiller and others incorporating heavy-duty shock cord to act as dampers.

On a reach they borrowed a variation of the Braine gear, which can be seen on most model yachts.

But for going to windward for long distances across the ocean something more sophisticated is required than tiller lines linked to the clews of headsails. Planning for the Single-Handed Transatlantic Race from Plymouth to New York in 1960 was just the impetus needed for the fertile minds of Francis Chichester and Colonel Blondie Hasler to lick the problem of keeping a small boat sailing efficiently to weather without having someone at the helm around the clock. Both came up with a vane on the transom which could be preset at a given apparent wind angle and directly linked to the rudder (or a trim tab). A quadrant at the base of the wind vane had crossover tiller lines so rigged that a tendency to luff up pulled

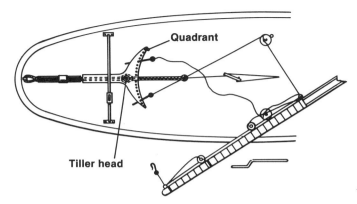

Quadrant

Tiller head

Braine's self-steering gear for model yachts

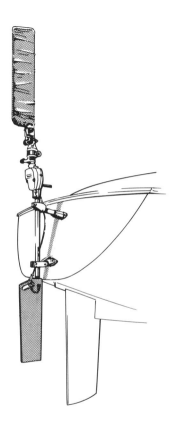

**Modern Wind Vane steering
attached to transom**

the tiller to weather, and vice versa. There were many variations on the theme, but the most popular was marketed as the
Hasler Self-Steering Gear.

When Blondie reached New York 48 days out in his 26-ft
junk-rigged Folkboat she had sailed herself for all but one hour
of the voyage and set the fashion for all solo navigators or those
sailing single-handed.

While vane-steering has the supreme attribute of not calling
for any source of power other than the wind, it has some
drawbacks. It is vulnerable to damage either by the seas or
while berthing. And it can hardly be said to enhance the
appearance of a boat. There are more compact versions of his
original idea still available today for the owner who does not
want to depend on electrical power. They cost around $1,300,
depending on the mounting brackets.

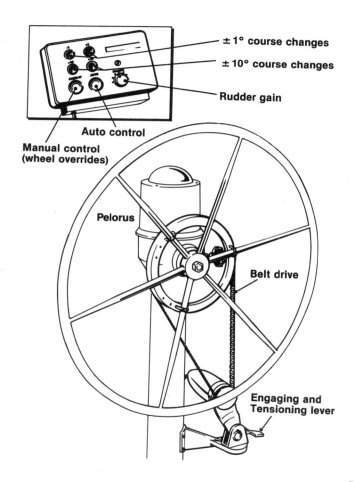

± 1° course changes

± 10° course changes

Rudder gain

Auto control

Manual control
(wheel overrides)

Pelorus

Belt drive

Engaging and
Tensioning lever

Autopilots

Whereas power-assisted autopilots have been standard in most motorboats whose owners aim to do more than tow water-skiers behind them, they have only taken off for sailing yachts in the past decade. One U.K. firm has supplied 180,000 units in that time and is still selling 1,500 annually.

It started with a simple athwartships push-pull rod snapped on to a stud on the tiller arm, taking its command from an ordered course monitored by its own transmitting compass (see p. 73).

A simple variation for wheel steering involves a toothed rubber belt-drive engaged to an inner sprocket secured to the ship's steering wheel, driven by its own control unit, usually mounted low down on the pedestal of the pelorus (see left), or on the side of the cockpit. There is a simple tensioning lever for engaging the belt-drive effectively.

Many feel that the need for an ordered course to steer in degrees throws up discrepancies with the steering compass. It is simple to put the boat on the desired course and then hit the "auto" button on the control unit. Adjustments can be made in 1° or 10° steps by pressing other buttons. Even the rudder action can be damped to suit your own boat's steering behavior. To disengage, there is a "stand-by" button; or you simply lift the piston unit off its locking stud on the tiller.

If you wish, the control panel can be duplicated by another on a remote lead. Also there is the option of a small wind vane to sail by apparent wind angle. Finally, there is a black box which will link the controls to any radio navigation system (Decca or Loran-C) and take you to the next way point.

In case the autopilot forgets itself, there is an off-course alarm system and overload protection. In all systems there is an upper limit to the weight of impact on the rudder the autopilot can handle. This is known as the "stall thrust." Each model has its designed limits, coupled with the maximum size

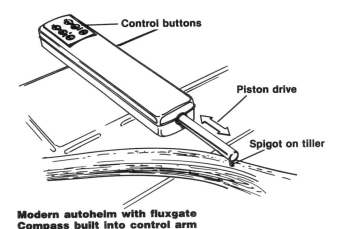

Control buttons

Piston drive

Spigot on tiller

**Modern autohelm with fluxgate
Compass built into control arm**

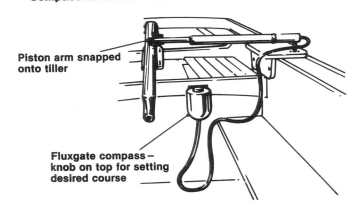

Piston arm snapped
onto tiller

Fluxgate compass –
knob on top for setting
desired course

Earlier auto-steering model

of boat it can handle. Makers vary in their claims for these limits. One has at the bottom end of its range a stall thrust of 160 lb (73 kg), suitable for boats up to 33 ft (10 m). Recently I sailed a Nicholson 36 with this same autopilot and found it did a fine job, although possibly the onset of limiting sea states and awkward wind angles came rather sooner than would the next model up the line: 300 lb (136 kg) stall thrust, suitable for boats up to 43 ft (13 m).

Another manufacturer offers to drive a 33-ft boat with $12\frac{1}{2}$ percent less thrust for a 42-ft boat. Here is another case for talking to an independent dealer or consultant.

Like most of today's advanced technology for boats, prices have come down with competition. The simplest push-pull system for a tiller costs a little over $300, while the wheel-steering autopilot is under $500, surprisingly, less than for a typical wind-operated vane steering.

The heart of this type of autopilot is a small gimballed fluxgate compass, no bigger than a golf ball. It is not a north-seeking magnetic compass in the conventional sense but keeps pointing to whatever relative heading is preset by the operator. The guts of it looks like an armature winding.

Power requirements
Whichever way you slice it, autopilots need electrical power behind them. It is safe to say that their average consumption is equivalent to having your navigation lights switched on. Nevertheless, if you don't keep a second battery isolated for starting your engine, you can flatten a battery overnight by running under autopilot with navigation lights switched on and no restrictions below. That is why a Beneteau 32 in which I was a guest last year had to sail into the lock at Ouistreham after an easy passage from Beaulieu, then hump the battery ashore for recharging and a long expensive lunch before going on to Caen. I recommend two 60 amp-hr batteries with a

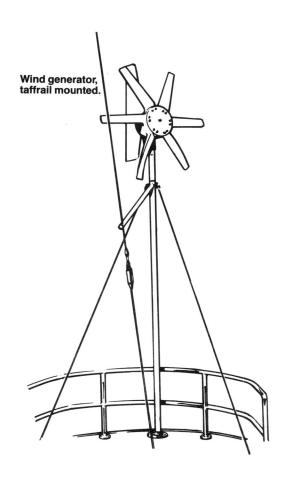

Wind generator, taffrail mounted.

simple selector switch enabling either or both to be put on load.

As any submariner will tell you, the signs of a DC battery at the top of its charge are that it should be gassing freely and show maximum voltage and electrolyte specific gravity readings (using a hygrometer). In a yacht there is generally only a voltmeter to indicate your battery's health. Once below 12 V (or 24 V, as the case may be) smack it on charge right away. A safe rule is to run the engine for an hour twice a day, even if your hotel load (fridge, lighting and navigation aids) is not restricted by the skipper's edict, which sometimes stretches to navigation lights being switched off in quiet waters.

Other sources of power independent of fossil fuels are the sun and wind. A typical single solar-energy plate in direct sunlight will give you about a 3-amp charge, but it costs nearly $750 and is not at its best in the clouds and fog associated with high latitudes.

A wind generator, which is a miniwindmill stuck on its own mast at the taffrail, will deliver 2 amps or 12 V in a steady 12 kt breeze rising to 6 amps in 30-kt winds at an installation cost of around $600. But it depends on relative wind strength, so may not be too effective in that dream cruise to Antigua along the edge of the Doldrums. One model (Aquair / Ampair) can double as a towed water turbine; it is especially suitable for fast downwind sailing in low relative wind speeds, claiming up to 8-amps charge.

Most occasional yacht navigators are put off enlisting the aid of the sun or the stars, let alone the moon or the planets, to fix their position by the very thought of trying to understand the theory behind the practice. Words like sidereal hour angle, the ephemerides, the first point of Aries and the rest of the jargon are daunting hurdles to be faced in a classroom, let alone in the wet cockpit of a yacht.

But you don't have to understand the theory of internal combustion engines to drive a car, or how a microprocessor works to check your bank balance at a cash machine. All you need to know are their modes of operation, their snags and practical limitations—and learn Osram's Law ("switch it on," first propounded by the Pakistani physicist, Professor O.S. Ram).

So, before you turn your back on a sextant and those overcrowded tables in a nautical almanac, which are about as confusing to read as a commuter timetable, join me in putting celestial navigation to work without relying on too much of the theory.

Which sextant?

This instrument, so-called because they used always to have a 60° graduated arc for reading off the altitude, will measure the observed angle above the horizon of the sun, moon or any other heavenly body and give the answer in degrees, minutes and seconds of arc (in practice, minutes and decimals: thus 33° 47.7' is 33 degrees 47 minutes and 42 seconds).

Don't rush in and blow up to $750 on the sort of alloy-framed sextant a U-boat commander used, although the Chinese have entered the market with a high-quality sextant at $275. Pause to determine what you really need from it. That in turn

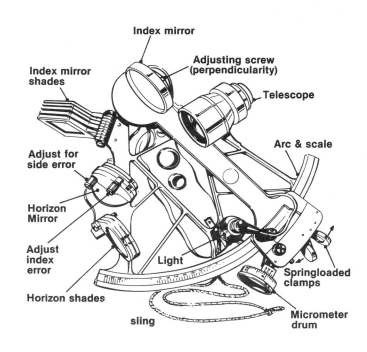

Index mirror

Adjusting screw (perpendicularity)

Index mirror shades

Telescope

Arc & scale

Adjust for side error

Horizon Mirror

Adjust index error

Light

Springloaded clamps

Horizon shades

Micrometer drum

sling

Professional sextant

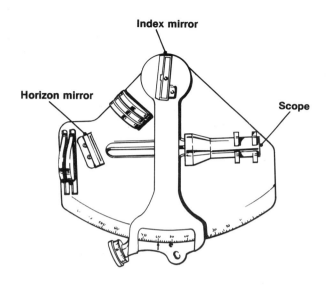

Index mirror

Horizon mirror

Scope

Beginner's sextant (solid plastic)

depends on the confidence you place in any altitude you measure under the conditions prevailing at sea in a yacht. Start with the firm intention that you will never waste your time taking sights when conditions are such that their results are of dubious value right from the first step; that is, in measuring the observed altitude. Master the sun shot in good conditions first before you even think about trying out a set of stars. Know what degree of confidence to invest in your efforts, always erring on the skeptical side.

You pay for what you get and, in some cases, what you do not need. The simplest and by far the cheapest sextant is one constructed around a flat heavy-duty plastic plate cut as the segment of a circle with 120° on its graduated lower arc. The index arm and its associated mirror rotate about the "center" of the imaginary circle, with a micrometer for fine reading of minutes of arc after having spring-locked the index arm onto the nearest degree. It costs less than $60.00 and is quite adequate for all the purposes listed above, with the following limitations:

(a) Its claimed accuracy is one minute, probably within the operating error of most beginners.

(b) Its telescope has only 1.5 magnification and a limited field of view, so locking onto and bringing stars down to the horizon will be that much more difficult.

(c) It is susceptible to considerable errors of alignment and must be checked on each occasion of use. (See below for sextant errors.) One I picked up the other day had so much side error that the direct and reflected images of the sun never met.

(d) It has no built-in lighting for reading off observed altitudes at dusk. But since you won't be relying on star sights, this inconvenience is acceptable.

(e) It has a limited set of shades (hinged filters which can be swung into your field of vision through either mirror to reduce glare).

Otherwise it serves its purpose and comes securely stowed within its own plastic box about 8 in square and 3 in deep. The sextant itself weights a little over a pound (0.75 kg).

Secondhand sextants

These are surprisingly hard to come by, considering the decline in the number of merchant ships in service. Occasionally the classified columns of a local newspaper in a seaport will have one, but the yachting press rarely advertises them. When it does, the more sophisticated professional models fetch up to $200 if bought direct, probably more from a chandler.

What to look for:

(a) Check both mirrors and the telescope for signs of damp. The mirrors can always be resilvered at little cost. If you leave blotchy patches on them the efficiency of the sextant falls off quickly.

(b) There should be a test certificate inside the lid of the box with the date and maximum error obtaining—usually negligible.

(c) Check for the errors listed below and be sure that the adjusting screws for eradicating them are operable.

(d) See that the lighting circuit is functioning.

(e) The sextant should be clamped in its stowage inside its box so that it does not rattle around when it is picked up.

(f) Make sure that the spring lock holds the index arm firmly on to the graduated arc.

(g) Go for a telescope with 3× or 5× magnification but don't bother with 8×30 monocular star scopes which cannot cope with the amount of movement usually prevailing.

Correcting errors

A sextant's accuracy depends on:

(a) Certain errors being allowed for or mechanically adjusted out of the way.

(b) Various corrections to allow for the observer's height of eye (above sea level) tabulated in your almanac.

(c) Special corrections for moon, planet or star shots, also from the tables.

(d) Having a reliable distant horizon from which to measure the altitude.

Since an error of one minute of arc can work its way onto your plotted position as one nautical mile, it is important to take all these into account, but especially the quality of the horizon. On a calm clear day with a sharp horizon easily showing where the sea ends and the sky begins and little or no movement on the boat there is no problem. But a hazy horizon and a watery sun observed from a bucking platform is where you must trust your own judgment on the attainable accuracy. Not only must you find the true horizon, if necessary waiting for the boat to lift on top of the swell, but the angle measured must be in the vertical plane. Your eye looks at the horizon through the lower glass, which has a mirror to one side picking up the body to be observed through the index mirror, so called because it is attached to the index arm on which the altitude measured is read in degrees and minutes.

In practice with the sun it is easy to swing the index arm in the direction of the reflected path of the sun on the surface until you have the lower limb (bottom edge) of the sun roughly on the horizon. Waggle the sextant from side to side until your observed lower limb just kisses the horizon (see p. 78) with an unchanged altitude setting.

If you are timing the sight, as you must for all but meridian passage shots (the moment when the observed body hangs stationary in the sky, generally nearing due south neither climbing nor falling), call "cut" or "mark" or whatever you have as agreed procedure with your assistant or, if you are using a stopwatch, press it for subsequent correlating with GMT.

In the days before inertial navigation and hyperbolic aids, aircraft navigators used "bubble" sextants with their own artificial horizon, but they are not stable enough for our purposes and are no longer available. On the eve of a Bermuda Race in pre-Loran-C days a hot ocean racing navigator showed me his special sextant with a prespun gyro inside its handle

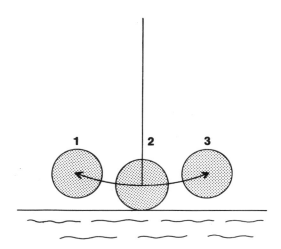

Slewing the sextant to get maximum altitude with the sextant vertical.

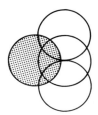

Checking side error by taking the reflected sun through the observed one

that forcibly restrained him if he tried measuring altitudes off the plumb vertical. When next seen after the usual broad reach down to Bermuda, he was making his landfall under spinnaker from the sou'west, having missed the island on his first pass.

The other errors must all be allowed for or corrected in this order:

Perpendicularity is a check to confirm that the index mirror is lying in the same plane as the sextant. Set the index arm around 60° against the scale on its arc and then look obliquely into the index mirror at the index arc and its reflected image.

If they don't form an uninterrupted line there is perpendicularity error which must be taken out by adjusting a setscrew on the back of the index mirror.

Side error occurs when the reflected and direct image of the sun are not in the same plane, due to the horizon glass being slightly out of plane. To check it, use as much color filter as you need to look straight at the sun, set the index arm on zero and turn the micrometer first one way and then the other. In the process the sun's reflected image will pass from above to below. If the reflective image does not coincide precisely with the direct sun (see above) the side error can be taken out by turning a screw in the center of the frame of the horizon glass.

Index error is present if the horizon glass is not parallel to the index glass when the sextant is set to read 0°00′. The simplest way of checking this is to look at any distant horizontal datum, such as the horizon, when it will be seen to have a step in, as in focusing with a modern camera. Turn the micrometer until the horizon forms a clean unbroken line. Then it will be seen that the index arm is reading a small amount either side of zero.

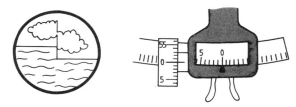

Horizon broken with sextant reading zero.

If it is to the *left* of the zero point, the error is said to be "on the arc" and the correction to be applied when reading off any observed altitude is *minus*.

If the index arm is to the *right* of zero, it is "off the arc" and the amount has to be *added* to the observed altitude.

If the amount is small (under three minutes) let it stand and just remember to apply it on all occasions. If it is a relatively large figure it should be eliminated by an adjusting screw at the base of the horizon glass frame. An index error of 1.5 minutes can be lived with, just so long as you remember that it represents 1½ nautical miles' error on your position line.

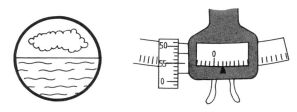

Horizon straight. Index error 2° off the arc (+)

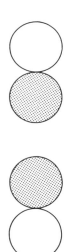

Reflected image above and under observed sun.

The above method is best checked by taking several observations breaking and then realigning the horizon.

In theory the most accurate method of finding index error is to eliminate side error as described above and then measure the sun's observed diameter as follows:

1. Get the reflected image sitting tangentially on top of the observed sun and read off the number of minutes on the arc.

2. Swing the reflected image down until it is now tangentially *under* the observed sun and read off the minutes off the arc.

79

What you have done is measured twice the diameter of the sun. The sun's monthly pages in the almanac give a lot of data: *inter alia,* its meridian passage, times of rising and setting and twilight and the measurement of the sun's *semidiameter* for each day, which varies between 15.8 and 16.3 minutes. (The reason it is listed is that the tables are computed on the assumption that you should be observing the *center* of the sun and not its upper or lower limb).

So your reading for index error should add up to four times the semidiameter, e.g.:

If the sun's semidiameter is listed as 15.8, its full diameter is 31.6 minutes and the sum total of your reading on and off the arc should amount to 63.2. The amount by which the two readings are biased either side of zero on the scale is your index error. Suppose you read 30.0 on the arc and 33.5 off it (totaling 63.5, which is near enough). Divide the total measured by two ($=31.8$) and you will see that the real zero point is $33.5-31.8$ *off the arc* $=1.7$ minutes, and your index error is $+1.7$.

Looking after the sextant

Whether it cost you $50 or $500, a sextant that is not cared for will soon reduce your self-confidence in the observations you take with it. Here are the dos and don'ts:

1. Have a permanent stowage for your sextant case, preferably built so that the lid can be opened and the instrument taken out or replaced *in situ.* It should be located in the driest part of the boat consistent with accessibility.
2. Never grab the sextant or hold it except by its handle.
3. Keep it secured to your person by a lanyard around your neck attached to the handle.
4. Have a loose-fitting plastic or other waterproof hood which you can slip over the sextant while it is exposed on deck and not actually shooting sights.

5. Dry it off immediately after use as gently as you can. Use lens paper to clean the mirrors and telescope, soft tissue for the frame of the instrument.
6. Keep the graduated arc lightly oiled.
7. Check the various errors on each occasion before use.
8. Have your telescope eyepiece focus point marked in some way so that no time is wasted looking through a blurred scope.

Times

At this point you need a broad understanding of the significance of the various kinds of time used in celestial navigation.

GMT remains the datum time from which all celestial navigation calculations are derived. Consolidated universal time (with its acronym luckily taken from the French as UTC) briefly flourished as an alternative designation but is no longer in use.

Zone time is an arbitrary adjustment of clock time to spread the hours of darkness more or less evenly either side of midnight. With a few exceptions (Iran $3\frac{1}{2}$ hours ahead of GMT, Newfoundland $3\frac{1}{2}$ hours behind), these adjustments are made in units of one hour, representing 15° of longitude spread $7\frac{1}{2}°$ either side of the meridian in the center of each time zone. So GMT extends from longitude 7°30′W. Bermuda in the vicinity of 65°W lies in the zone either side of 60°W (52°30W to 67°30W) which is 4 hours behind GMT.

Local time is zone time corrected to take account of any local variations such as daylight saving time, usually one hour added to give longer evenings.

Time Signals

WWV Fort Colorado puts out GMT time signals every minute interspersed by navigation warnings on 2.5, 5, 10, 15, 20 and

25 MHz voice. WWVH from Hawaii does the same, omitting 25 MHz. This signal is also available on a battery-powered dedicated Sony receiver with its own whip antenna.

EST is given continuously from Canada on CHU, using 3.33, 7.335 and 14.670 MHz.

EST and GMT are also available by telephone, at (900) 410-8463. BBC World Service on different shortwave frequencies gives GMT on the hour every hour.

Most local radio stations give the time when they've nothing better to say; all right for calling the watch below, but not for astro-nav.

Ship's time is simply the time kept on the ship's clock which governs the change of watches and mealtimes. On a long W-E passage there is always some competition among the watch-keepers for when the crossing of each Time Zone should be put into effect (the equitable solution is to shave $\frac{1}{2}$ hour off each of two night watches). Most airline passengers adjust their wristwatches on takeoff to the local time of the next stopover, but round-trip commuters to New York by Concorde resolutely keep London time in the eternal battle to stave off jet lag.

Greenwich hour angle (GHA) is an east-to-west measurement of the sun's position relative to the Greenwich meridian as seen from the earth's center at any given moment. It is tabulated from 0°–360° for every one or two hours on the monthly sun pages in any almanac, with corrections for intervening times.

At 1400 GMT the GHA of the sun on January 14, 1987, was 31°08.3. If the time of observation had been 15.11.42 the sun's GHA correction table for 1 hr 11 mins 42 is 17°55.5, making the GHA at that time 31°08.3 + 17°55.0 = 49°03.3.

Local hour angle (LHA) is the hour angle measured from the longitude on which the observer happens to be, also measured in degrees to the westward (or clockwise around the globe). LHA is found by:

If your longitude is West, *adding* it to the GHA. If your longitude is East, *subtracting* it from the GHA.

Hereabouts use a little ploy with 360° (or multiples) being a wild card to be added or subtracted as necessary to make the sum fit the tables.

In an E longitude 360° can be deducted if the LHA comes to over 360°.

In a W longitude 360° may be added to the GHA if needed to give a high enough figure for subtraction.

Other definitions

Geographical position (GP) is the spot on the earth's surface directly under any heavenly body, assuming a line drawn from it to the earth's center.

The GP at any given moment can be measured EW by its LHA and NS by its declination:

Declination (Dec) is the latitude of the GP N or S of the equator. In the case of the sun, when it is furthest away from those of us who sail in northern waters, it will reach latitude 23°S in midwinter and about six months later reach latitude 23°N. As the sun crossed the equator with declination zero we have the spring and autumn equinoxes (equal period of daylight and night) usually associated with equinoctial gales, although it seems to me there is little more truth in that assertion than saying it is always rough in the Bay of Biscay. In nautical almanacs the declination is said to have the *same name* as the latitude when both are N or S; but a *contrary name* when they are not (e.g., Lat 40°N dec 12°S is a *contrary name*).

Zenith distance (ZD)   When you measure the altitude of the sun it is the angle observed between the horizon and the sun after making various corrections already noted. For the purpose of calculating one's latitude from a noon sight, it is necessary to work from the complement of your observed altitude: 90° minus altitude, since we we have to deal with a latitude scale running from 0° at the equator to 90° at the pole, and not the other way round.

Azimuth is the true bearing of any heavenly body. It can most accurately be determined by special alt-azimuth tables, but may also be obtained by visual observation if the altitude is not too high.

Taking a sight and working it out
Books, tables and methods
To work out a celestial sight (or "reduce it," as they say), there are certain publications which you must have, unless you have a programmed computer to do the job for you. Those most commonly found on the navigator's shelf are:

The *Nautical Almanac* for the current year, issued by U.S. Government Printing Office, Washington, D.C.

H.O. 249 *Sight Reduction Tables for Air Navigation*

H.O. 229 *Sight Reduction Tables for Marine Navigation*
  (1) covers from equator-latitude 15° N and S. Mouth of the Amazon to the Windward Islands.
  (2) covers latitudes 15°–30° N or S. Leeward Islands and Gulf of Mexico, Dakar to Canary Islands.
  (3) covers latitudes 30°–45° N and S. Jacksonville to Halifax, Madeira to the Gironde.
  (4) covers latitudes 45°–60° N and S. The British Isles, Bordeaux to Bergen, Halifax to Cape Farewell, Greenland.

Reed's Nautical Almanac for the current year.

Depending on which tables you use there are various pads of Sight Reduction forms which keep your calculations moving step-by-step in an orderly manner. The Admiralty's NP 400(a) is suitable for use with any of them. *Reed's* presents its tables in a sharply different method which may seem unfamiliar at first, but is explained in the text.

Use of Calculators
There are many different methods of reducing sights by using hand-held scientific calculators to produce all the answers without the chore of having to enter too many tables, add up or subtract.

The Nav-Tech Corporation among others offers a hand-held calculator so programmed that the user need enter no tables whatsoever. He needs only the sextant altitude and time of observation. Another simple system is the Simanda Astro-Navigation Kit* which gives you a sextant of sorts, a scientific calculator, *Reed's Almanac* and a readily comprehensible step-by-step guide on how to do it—all for less than $100. If you already have a sextant and *Reed's*, the calculator and the methodology cost just $30.

Nursery slopes—two sights to master
  (1) *Meridian Altitude—the noon sight* The first and easiest sight to measure is the sun's altitude at the moment of its meridian passage: that is when it crosses your meridian of longitude either due north or due south of you. You can work out when this will happen by reference to the monthly Sun tables in the Nautical Astronomy section of *Reed's Almanac* or other almanacs and in Admiralty or U.S. equivalents. It is listed as either "Transit" or "Mer-Pass." Since Greenwich Mean Time is an average based on 24 hours for each 365 days of the year, meridian passage seldom occurs precisely at noon GMT even on the meridian of Greenwich. The tables show the sun's meridian passage can be a few minutes (up to fourteen) early or late on 1200 GMT.

Having obtained the time of Mer-Pass, say, 1208, then you

* Obtainable from Simanda Yachting Services, 8 Grovelands, Lower Bourne, Farnham, Surrey GU103RQ.

must correct it for whatever distance you happen to be located yourself off the prime meridian. To do this, convert arc of longitude into time by the simple formula that each degree is equivalent to four minutes of time. If you are to the east of Greenwich you will get Mer-Pass early, as indeed you get sunrise earlier as you fly east toward Europe from the United States. If, for example, you are off Newport, Rhode Island, in longitude 71°W your correction will be $71 \times 4 = 284$ minutes later and your time of meridian passage will be $1208 + 0444W = 1652$ GMT (or 1152 EST). There are converting tables in the almanacs for arc into time, in case the above is beyond the scope of your mental abacus or pocket calculator.

A Mer-Alt shot as it is called is easier to hit off if you have the time of its happening worked out beforehand, but it is not necessary. Nor need you worry if your estimated position is doubtful, since you need to be over fifteen minutes of longitude out before you affect the issue by a minute of time. Often it is necessary to get the helmsman to come off course (either

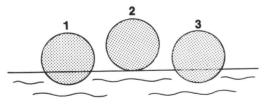

Sextant altitude at meridian passage.
1 Sun's image before meridian passage
2 At meridian passage
3 Shortly after meridian passage with altitude decreasing

to get the spinnaker or jib out of the sextant's field of view or, simply, to allow the navigator to take his sight without being doused by heavy spray). So an accurate prediction of the time of meridian passage is helpful.

It is not strictly necessary, because you can get your sight by watching the sun's altitude climb and slow down briefly to hang stationary in the sky before the altitude starts to drop again (see drawing at left). You just read the altitudes until you have passed their peak, then take the time and log reading.

Bringing it back alive Since you'll need both hands to use the sextant, first brace yourself securely standing up so that you can bring the sun down clear of the rig. Leaning back against the main boom is one option, but *always* clip on with a safety harness, even in calm weather. It is surprising how much uneven movement a boat has in calm seas. A friend of mine lost his life taking a noon shot on a westward trade wind crossing to the Caribbean. An unseen, lazy swell caught the boat and her navigator off-balance. The motor did not start first touch, and there was so little wind that the watch on deck could not lower the drooping spinnaker and get back to him soon enough.

Sometimes it pays to have another member of the crew hold onto you as you take the sight.

Before taking the sight, determine your height of eye at the moment of shooting (usually 10–12 feet in a typical yacht). This will be used to enter the Total Altitude Correction Table to cover all sextant corrections except index error.

At 12 ft and an observed altitude of 35° the correction for a lower limb (LL) shot will be $+11.4$ (interpolated between 30° and 40°). If it was taken in June, July or August there is a further minuscule correction of -0.2, making your final figure $+11.2$.

Now the working is easy. For a sight taken in N latitudes:

Sextant altitude	36°07.8
Index error (say)	−2.8
	36°05.0
LL alt correction	+11.2
Corrected altitude	36°16.2
ZD (90° − alt)	53°43.8
Dec N (same)	8°38.6
Latitude	62°22.4N

Note the final addition of 43.8 and 38.6 minutes ends up as 82.4, which is 1° carried forward and 22.4 minutes, there being 60 minutes to a degree. If the Dec had been S (contrary) it would have been subtracted from ZD making the latitude 45°05.2N.

That's all there is to it. The end result is that you have your latitude fixed beyond doubt within your personal error of sight-taking and any errors you have not properly taken out of the sextant itself (see p. 77). Even among skilled navigators in perfect conditions individual errors can amount to 0.75 minutes, which is ¾ mile.

(2) *Sun Sight—the single-position line* This will put you on a line at right angles to the bearing (azimuth) of the sun, somewhere on which your position lies. On its own it's no better than a single compass bearing of a known feature on the coastline.

The data required before reducing the sight are:

(a) Your DR position at the time of taking the sight. This need not be very accurate.

(b) The True Altitude (H_0) of your sextant shot after applying all the necessary corrections, as in taking the Mer-Alt sight.

(c) The time (GMT) at which the sight was taken accurate to ± 2 secs, well within the scope of any quartz crystal watch with a recent time check behind it.

(d) For future reference, but not needed for the working, note the log reading and the bearing of the sun.

(e) The assumed latitude, rounded off to the degree nearest to your DR latitude.

(f) The assumed longitude needed to round off the computation of LHA so as to get rid of its minutes of arc. This may be some distance from your DR longitude but don't worry, it'll all come out in the wash.

(g) The declination appropriate for the GMT of the sight.

The sextant altitude used must be precisely on the GMT at which it was taken. The best way is to take several shots, each carefully timed, and end up with an ironed-out average. This introduces an area of potential error which does not apply to Mer-Alt sights, in which the altitude is read off when the sun has stopped ascending, and no time is needed.

If possible, always use the same crew member to note the times of your shots. It sounds simple enough, but it is surprising how many people get flustered and make silly mistakes. It is better not to let your timekeeper use his own watch, but either give him one with a known error from a recent time signal or, better still, a stopwatch.

All he has to do is wait for you to say "Stand by . . . cut!" (or "mark!" in an American boat), then write down the time in minutes and seconds, followed by the sextant angle in degrees and minutes of arc to a single place of decimals as called by you. Always make him repeat the sextant altitude back to you before going on to take the next altitude, which again is noted against the time. How many observations you take for a single sight is dependent on the quality of the horizon and your own confidence. Unless the cloud cover or sea conditions make me accept less, I never take fewer than three shots.

The most popular way of averaging out altitudes and times is by adding them both up and dividing by the number of observations, probably using a calculator. But the best way is to plot all of them against their times on squared paper, as in the diagram on the right. To do this the timekeeper starts his stopwatch at the first "cut," which is later plotted as an x against zero time, with the others then plotted out against stopwatch time in the same manner. Then draw a straight line which most closely caters for all the x-marks on the graph paper. From it you can choose any convenient altitude and time as inputs for working out the sight.

First you have to check the GMT of your stopwatch zero by stopping it against a time signal or clock of known accuracy.

The example in the diagram shows that the altitude chosen to work from is 2.3 minutes of arc at variance with the one which a calculator would have arrived at by averaging out the "cuts." The reason is that the calculator took each altitude at face value and included one wild one which was obviously inaccurate, whereas the line drawn across the graph paper ignored that one. In some cases that could mean a discrepancy of over 2 miles in the position line and, therefore, the fix ultimately obtained with a second sight later.

Working it Out

Using modern tables it is no more difficult than reconciling your checkbook stubs against your bank balance. If you use a sight reduction form, it is even easier. The following is an

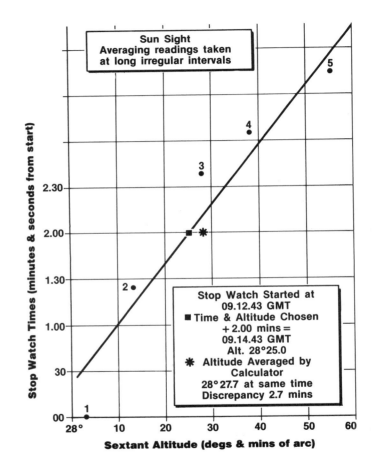

Sun Sight
Averaging readings taken
at long irregular intervals

Stop Watch Times (minutes & seconds from start)

Sextant Altitude (degs & mins of arc)

Stop Watch Started at
09.12.43 GMT
■ Time & Altitude Chosen
+ 2.00 mins =
09.14.43 GMT
Alt. 28°25.0
✳ Altitude Averaged by
Calculator
28°27.7 at same time
Discrepancy 2.7 mins

abridged form, since the corrections to time and sextant altitude are assumed to have been done in your head or on a scratch pad.

Date   15 July 19—

DR position	49°48N	05°42W
GMT	08h.46m 01s	The time has been averaged out and any corrections applied.
GHA sun	298° 32.1'	Taken from *Nautical Almanac* for exact hour = 0800.
Increment	11° 30.0'	From Sun GHA Correction tables for 46 mins 01 secs.
GHA	310° 02.1'	
Assumed longitude (W)	6° 02.1'	Long. W is subtracted; E is added. The assumed longitude arbitrarily chosen near the DR so as to end up with LHA reading in degrees only, no minutes of arc.
LHA sun	304° 00.0'	
Assumed longitude 50° N		Nearest exact longitude to the DR.
Declination	N 21° 35.2'	From *Nautical Almanac*, interpolating d between Decs for successive days. See note on increments below.
Tab alt(H$_c$)	38° 01.7'	All corrections applied, inc height of eye for tables.
True alt(H$_o$)	37° 54.9'	In this case H$_c$ is the greater, otherwise it would be Towards.
Intercept	6.8'	
	Away	Co:125° Sp:7kts (var)
Azimuth (bearing) 102°		
Log reading, say 62.8		

Increments The small "d" which crops up in the tables is for the difference between successive entries. In some cases the figure is so small that you can allow for it by eye. In this case the Dec for 0800 is N21°35.6; for 1000 it is N21°34.9, a difference of only 0.7'. But "d" is a significant factor in arriving at the Tab Alt(H$_c$). You first take out the altitude for the degrees of declination (N 21°) and must then adjust to take account of the 35.2'. The Alt-Az Tables as they are sometimes known are entered for the assumed longitude (50°N) in the same "name" as the declination (i.e., N), LHA of 304° against Dec of 21°. The information supplied is H$_c$37°35.8' with d as + 44.2 and the azimuth as 102°.

The d figure is simply the difference between Dec 21° and Dec 22°. There are interpolation tables with instructions which are comprehensible. Or use a calculator to work out how much of d + 44.2 you have to apply for the 35.2' of declination:

$$\frac{35.2}{60} \times 44.2 = 25.9$$

On obtaining the intercept, if the corrected observed altitude (H$_o$) is greater than the tabulated altitude (H$_c$), the intercept is *toward* the sun's azimuth shown above. If H$_c$ is the greater the intercept is *away* from the sun's bearing. Just remember: "True Greater Toward."

Plotting the Sight
(1) Plot the *assumed* latitude and longitude used in the working above.
(2) Draw the azimuth (bearing) from that latitude-longitude position and mark off the intercept as miles using the latitude scale on the plot.
(3) A line drawn at right angles through the intercept point is your position line.

When you get your next sight, you can run it on, exactly as in a running fix using single compass bearings at intervals so spaced as to give you a cut of 30° or more. This will give you a sun-run-sun observed position or, more simply, a fix. The following example uses a meridian altitude sight as the second position line (see p. 88). The plot next to it is one taken on the 1984 Bermuda Race.

The moon: a little more difficult

Because it is the fastest celestial body in the sky (at 2,400 mph), and its high rate of change of bearing and altitude call for fiddling corrections to the sextant readings, the moon is not everybody's favorite. But it's there, and on about fifteen days each month available for a simultaneous shot with the sun. In fact, only when it is full is it unseen by day, since it rises around sunset and sets at dawn. During half the rest of the month it appears as a waxing segment, getting steadily bigger from its first appearance as a sliver of a new moon, until it goes out as an old moon on the wane.

To distinguish between the two, remember the italic letter *x*. The waxing moon comes first and has its clearly defined visible edge to the right as you look at it. Once on the wane, its hard perimeter is on the left. The waxing half-moon rises around midday and has its meridian passage near sunset, so it is an ideal afternoon sight, when the sun is in the western part of the sky. The waning half-moon will be in its meridian about sunrise and set at noon, so is suitable for a simultaneous sun-moon shot in the forenoon.

The tables allow you to take an observation either when its Upper Limb is tangential to the horizon (and the rest of it below) or with the Lower Limb on the horizon, as in a normal sun sight. Near its various quarters the moon appears to be canted, so that it is necessary to take an Upper Limb sometimes to be sure of not getting a false altitude by measuring the partly hidden lower sector of the moon.

Because it is so much nearer to the earth, its relative movement is quicker than any other heavenly body, so accurate timekeeping and recording are essential. But you seldom have glare on the horizon from which you are measuring its altitude, so can usually shoot without shades over either mirror or the sextant telescope.

Given modern tables in the nautical almanacs, and special care in taking the sight, there is no reason why the moon has traditionally been regarded as a fickle friend of yacht navigators.

All nautical almanacs have separate correction tables for Apparent Sextant Angle, GHA moon and the moon's declination.

The GHA may be tabulated hourly, four times a day (*Reed's*) or three times a day. Suppose the moon was taken at nearly the same time as the sun shot in the example above, say, 08 h.52 m.23 s on 15 July. Then

GHA for 0600 is	28°58.8′	with variation listed as 14° 30.3
add for 2 hours	+ 14°29.0′	(Moon GHA Corrn table for 1–6 hrs)
for 52 mins	+ 12°34.0	(Moon GHA Corrn table for up to 1 hr)
for 23 secs	+ 5.6′	
GHA for 08.52.23 is	56°07.4′	

When it comes to taking out the declination, see by inspection of the tables whether the corrections should be added or subtracted, depending on whether the next figure is greater or lesser.

Declination for 0600	S 5°24.8′	16.6 variation per hour noted

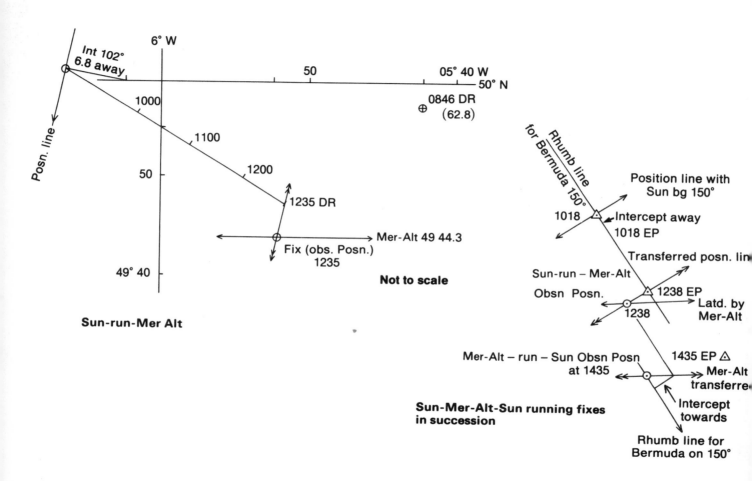

6° W

Int 102°
6.8 away

50

05° 40 W
50° N

1000

0846 DR
(62.8)

Posn. line

1100

1200

1235 DR

50

Mer-Alt 49 44.3

Fix (obs. Posn.)
1235

49° 40

Not to scale

Sun-run-Mer Alt

Rhumb line
for Bermuda 150°

Position line with
Sun bg 150°

1018

Intercept away
1018 EP

Transferred posn. lin

Sun-run – Mer-Alt

Obsn Posn.

1238 EP

Latd. by
Mer-Alt

1238

Mer-Alt – run – Sun Obsn Posn
at 1435

1435 EP

Mer-Alt
transferre

Intercept
towards

**Sun-Mer-Alt-Sun running fixes
in succession**

Rhumb line for
Bermuda on 150°

Subtract for 2 hours		
2 × 16.6	− 33.2′	
For 52 m 23 s	− 15.5′	(From Moon Dec Corrn tables)
Declination at		
08 h.52 m23 s is	S 4°36.1′	

Sextant Altitude Each almanac has its own system for applying moon altitude total corrections to apparent altitude. They all have explanatory notes. First you must enter the monthly page for the moon's times of rising and setting. There you will find the horizontal parallax figure for the day, probably between 54.1 and 61.0.

Then enter the moon altitude table with the observed altitude (sextant altitude corrected for index error) and horizontal parallax figure, taking care to use the correct half of the page of Upper or Lower Limb. From that you get a correction + or − to observed altitude; then you must make a further correction to height of eye, since the tables have been computed for 100 feet above sea level and have a special correction table to bring the observation down to the height at which you took it. Thus:

The moon's Upper Limb was taken at 08.52 on 15 July with 12 ft height of eye (HE) as 24°50.0′. The horizontal parallax (HP) was 59.3.

Moon's UL	24°50.0′
Correction	+ 25.3′
HE	+ 6.4′
True alt	25°21.7′

From this point on, the working and plotting is the same as for a single position line from a sun sight.

Star sights: counterproductive?

I rate simultaneous star shots at morning or evening twilight as not worth the bother. In ideal conditions—so rarely found in a yacht—a set of stars with Polaris (the feeble but easily found North Star) and three other correctly identified stars will give you an instant fix of potentially high reliability; but typically you find yourself cold and wet on deck at night with five-eighths cloud and only fleeting glimpses of your pre-selected stars between showers of cold seawater.

Naturally the quality of the horizon degenerates quickly at dusk, while the stars themselves melt away at dawn. The whole business of sitting around waiting to fire from the hip is tedious not only for the navigator but also for his chosen timekeeper. Then there follows the chore of working it all out. Robin Knox-Johnson sailed 27,000 miles around the world in 313 days without taking a star sight except on rare occasions for fun or to pass the time. Nor did Commander Bill King in "Galway Blazer."

If you are determined, or curious, to find out for yourself, there is no better book on the subject than Mary Blewitt's *Celestial Navigation for Yachtsmen*, first published in the reign of George VI but constantly updated, excepting only that the target reader implied by the title has now been changed to Yachtspersons. Her examples are all worked using the *Nautical Almanac* and AP 3270—*Sight Reduction Tables for Air Navigation*, Volume I.

The sextant as a rangefinder

The sextant can also be brought on deck for other uses than hacking down celestial bodies. It is by far the most accurate rangefinder available on board. Given the height of a lighthouse or daymark you can read off the vertical sextant angle and refer to any almanac for a conversion table giving range. A simultaneous bearing of the object yields an accurate and instantaneous fix. The tables are intended for use up to 7 miles. A glance at the tables shows why:

Take the Eddystone lighthouse (133 ft) with its light 41 meters above the sea. At 6-miles range its vertical sextant angle is only 12 seconds; an error of observation of 3 seconds would put you a mile out of position. Obviously index error must be applied. But it can be invaluable if struggling to round a headland in a fickle wind and foul tide by setting the sextant on its highest point and using it to show whether progress is being made or lost.

The same technique can be used against other yachts while racing.

See also horizontal sextant fixes on pages 48, 49.

Ability to cope with the weather as it comes is a major part of the navigator's problem. The very word covers a host of overlapping factors from visibility to moisture content, wind speed to sea-state, air and sea temperatures, to the passage of depressions with their associated fronts and the effects of ocean currents.

You may enjoy the weather and derive great assistance from the trade winds. Or you can be terrified while suffering unimaginable discomfort from it, be weather-bound, look weather-beaten or have trouble getting to weather of a hazard. The very word is all-pervading, dominating every moment of a sailor's life, especially if he is in a small underpowered yacht.

The strength and direction of the wind most concerns those who sail in tall ships, as Cruiser Trewsbury found once he cast off from the sinking Clipper *Blackgauntlet* in her longboat:

Hitherto [in clipper ships] he had dealt with the wind . . . wrestling to use it and master its power and fury. Now [in an open boat] the real enemy was the seething leaping and appalling water, so close at hand. All that waste of tumult was the enemy . . . about to pounce.
　　　—from John Masefield's immortal *Bird of Dawning*.

So it is with yachts. A maxi concerns itself mainly with using the wind to best advantage, but the smaller the yacht and the shorter its sail plan the more it must recognize the sea as the element to respect most.

There are well-attested formulas showing the relationship between wind and sea, but the fine print under them usually warns that they relate to conditions offshore. Local weather, tides and shoal water can produce seas which are not theoretically possible in the windspeed prevailing. The start of the 1951 Fastnet was delayed for six hours, during which the sou'westerly gale gusted 68 knots at Calshot and all small classes' racing was abandoned, but not before the Dragons had gone out and one was sunk without trace off the Castle. The crew of Gerald Potter's new Laurent Giles-designed *Fandango* (33 ft 6 in LWL) passed the time visiting a friend's boat on an adjacent mooring in the Roads, the lovely Nicholson-designed *Old Fox*. The rain was so heavy and her deckheads leaked so badly that we wore sou'westers and oilskins as we sat in her saloon and drank the owner's vintage Krug.

When we at last were sent away, the beat down the Solent was under a full ebb tide. Here we suffered not so much from the height of the seas (probably 12 ft off Hurst Castle) as the short interval (or period, as it's called) between them. Due to a combination of shallow water and wind-against-tide, the seas were vicious, steep and tumbling in one after the other. The book says that offshore there would have been over 20 seconds between successive wave tops, each of them 500 yards apart. On this occasion the wave interval was probably not much over three seconds and they were two to three boatlengths. The bone-shaking slamming was worse than anything I ever experienced in an offshore powerboat race. One of the crew then went to use the heads in the forepeak, a beautiful glazed porcelain bowl with a violet flower pattern and gleaming varnished seat, probably left over from a batch run up for the old Royal Yacht *Victoria & Albert*. At the critical moment the whole bowl disintegrated, leaving only a jagged porcelain stump. Fortunately I was gripping an overhead grabrail at the time, so was left swinging precariously, but still entire, over its razor-sharp remains. The next time I saw a head pan like that was on an Aeroflot flight from Moscow to Tbilisi, but I would expect to find one on the Orient Express. Neither the Russian copy of our Comet nor the Wagon-Lit coaches shuttling down to Venice is designed to pull the number of g's we did, probably 7 negative.

The point of the story is that once we were clear of the Needles and beating far to the south of Portland Bill, the tide turned foul and the seas flattened out even though the wind was still over 50 knots. Or so we guessed, having no anemometer in those days.

The bottom affects the wave size and behavior once the depth of water is under half the length of the waves. Much was written about the part played by the Labadie Bank in the 1979 Fastnet disaster, even though the official inquiry discounted it. The least depth on the bank is 200 ft. A wave behaves like a shallow-water one breaking over a sandbank when its length is 25 times the depth of water. On that day in August the waves would have had to be a mile long to fall into that category as they swept over the bank. In fact they were about 200 yds long and 20 ft high, rolling majestically in an ESE'ly direction when we surfed across it. Its main significance at that point is that it stands up like an underwater island from surrounding water of 400 ft in depth, so the echosounder fix crossed with a radio D/F bearing on Round Island 75 miles away is a good start for planning an accurate landfall at the Bishop Rock.

Anyway the yachts which got into trouble were all far to the east of the Labadie Bank in water deeper than 300 feet. But, like the Bermuda Triangle, the myth will persist as long as there is oil in the saloon lamp.

Other dangerous sea states outside their context are to be found in the confluence of tidal streams off a headland, such as where the Labrador current meets the Gulf Stream. Cape Sable, Hatteras, Barfleur, St Alban's Point and the Lizard can all give the navigator trouble and dump cook's curried stew onto the cabin sole, even though they are not as notorious as Portland Bill or the Alderney Race.

So, when planning a voyage, don't think you have all the weather data you need just by listening to the weather forecast. Use the tide to your advantage and comfort. Whenever there is the option and the current is significant, aim to set out during a wind-with-tide situation, which will give you six hours of relatively easy motion (and therefore faster sailing) than you would with wind against tide.

Scales and other definitions

The most famous yardstick for measuring wind and sea states is the 1805 Beaufort Scale named after the Hydrographer of the Navy in early Victorian days, Rear-Admiral Sir Francis Beaufort (1774–1857), a man of many parts, since he was the first to observe and codify the changing pattern of magnetic variations all over the world.

Notes to chart, p. 93: Wind speeds are taken at 33 ft above sea level.

The approximate wave heights and periods given are clear of the land. In shallow water both can be substantially different, as discussed earlier. These are average wave heights. For the maximum liable to be encountered, add half again. Thus waves in wind force 8 should be 18 ft from crest to trough, but the rogue wave in the same wind strength could be 25 ft.

BEAUFORT SCALE

Force	Wind Speed in kts	Wind Condition	Sea Conditions	Approx Wave ht feet	(meters)	Sea State	Period (secs)
0	0–1	Calm	Smooth, mirror-like sea.	—			
1	1–3	Light Air	Scale-like ripples; no foam crests.	$\frac{1}{4}$		0	
2	4–6	Light Breeze	Short wavelets; glassy crests; non-breaking.	$\frac{1}{2}$	(0.2)	1	
3	7–10	Gentle Breeze	Large wavelets; glassy crests, some breaking; occasional white foam.	2	(0.6)	2	3
4	11–16	Moderate Breeze	Small waves becoming longer; frequent white foam crests.	$3\frac{1}{2}$	(1)	3	4
5	17–21	Fresh Breeze	Moderate waves with more pronounced long form; many white foam crests; some spray.	6	(1.8)	4	5
6	22–27	Strong Breeze	Large waves form; white foam crests everywhere; probably more spray.	$9\frac{1}{2}$	(2.9)	5 6	6 7
7	28–33	Near Gale	Sea heaps up; white foam from breaking waves is blown in streaks with the wind.	$13\frac{1}{2}$	(4)		10 11
8	34–40	Gale	Moderately high waves with greater length; edges of crests break into spindrift; foam is blown in well-defined streaks with the wind.	18	(5.5)	7	
9	41–47	Strong Gale	High waves; crests of waves start to topple and roll over; spray may affect visibility.	23	(7)	8 9	15 18
10	48–55	Storm	Very high waves; overhanging crests; resulting foam is blown in dense white patches with the wind; sea surface takes on a whiter look; the tumbling of the sea becomes heavy and shock-like; visibility affected.	29	(8.8)		20
11	56–63	Violent Storm	Exceptionally high waves; sea covered with long white patches of foam blown in direction of wind; all wave crests are blown into froth; visibility affected.	37	(11.4)		23
12	64 +	Hurricane	Air is filled with spray and foam; sea is completely white with driving spray; visibility seriously affected.	45	(13.5)		25

Sea states are commonly quoted in North America but are never used in weather bulletins in Britain. Unfortunately they do not equate with wind forces. The following table gives a more precise relationship:

Sea state	Wave height
2	1½–3½ ft (0.5–1.0 m)
3	3½–5½ ft (1.0–2.3 m)
4	5½–7½ ft (1.6–2.3 m)
5	7½–13 ft (2.3–4 m)
6	13–18 ft (4–6 m)
7	18–42 ft (6–13 m)
8	42–65 ft (13–20 m)
9	65–130 ft (20–40 m)

Temperature scales

Converting degrees Fahrenheit to Centigrade

My rule of thumb is to double the Centigrade reading and add 30 to get the Fahrenheit equivalent, but this table may be more accurate:

°F	0	5	10	15	20	25	30	35	40	45	50
°C	−18	−15	−12	−9.4	−6.7	−4	−1	1.7	4.4	7.2	10

°F	55	60	65	70	75	80	85	90	95	100
°C	12.8	15.6	18.3	21	24	26.7	29.4	32.2	35	37.7

The exact ratio is

$$\text{Degrees Fahrenheit} = \frac{9}{5} \times \text{degrees Centigrade} + 32$$

Effective temperature

The wind has a measurable effect on the temperature you feel, as anyone sailing off the coast of Maine will tell you. The following table gives a fair indication of the wind-chill factor. The numbers should be added or subtracted from the temperature noted in a sheltered spot, measured in degrees Fahrenheit.

| Wind Speed | | | | Temperature (°F) | | | |
mph	(kts)	+30	+20	+10	0	−10	−20
10	(9)	+16	+ 2	− 9	−22	−31	−45
20	(17)	+ 3	− 9	−24	−40	−52	−68
30	(26)	− 2	−18	−33	−49	−63	−78
40	(35)	− 4	−22	−36	−54	−69	−87
50	(44)	− 7	−24	−38	−56	−70	−88

The barometer

Barometric scales

Nowdays the barometric pressure reported in the U.K. is always in millibars (mbs). But it was not always thus. Indeed the United States still talk of "inches of mercury" and even modern barometers show the pressure both in mbs and inches. Less frequently the pressure may be quoted in millimeters (mm) of mercury. Here is a scale. In case you lose it, 1 in of mercury = 34 mbs.

Inches	Mbs	Mms
28.05	950	712
28.35	960	719
28.65	970	727
28.05	980	738
29.23	990	743
29.52	1000	749
29.81	1010	757
30.12	1020	764
30.41	1030	772
30.71	1040	779
31.00	1050	787

The center of a depression or *Low* is commonly about 970 mbs, while the famous Azores *High* which is supposed to drift northwards in summer to let us stow away foul-weather gear occasionally is often around 1030 mbs. But don't be startled to hear 1005 quoted as a *Low*; it may well be if it is paired off with a *High* of 1040 in the same part of the world.

The old mercurial barometer housed in a black tube and secured vertically to a bulkhead on gimbals is now only seen

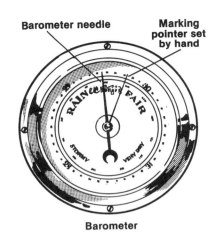

Barometer

in museums, pubs, the porch of a retired admiral's house or antique shops.

Nowadays aneroid barometers with a single needle show the pressure on a scale marked off clockwise, generally from around 900 to 1050 mbs. Often the inches are shown on a concentric scale with such time-honored but fatuous bromides as "Set Fair" around 1040 mbs through "Change" to "Stormy" at 960 mbs. There is a second and shorter pointer which can be used to set manually against the sensitive needle. The idea is that you tap the face of the barometer and the needle overcomes any friction to enable it to show the correct pressure at the time. The other pointer will then show whether the pressure has gone up or down since it was last set.

In a boat it is a good idea to read the barometer every hour at sea and enter the reading in the log, but only reset the pointer at much longer intervals, say every four or six hours. Otherwise every passing crew member will reset it each time he reads it and you are not left with a sufficiently clear indication of the pressure behavior.

To be pedantic, the barometer should be adjusted to read correctly at sea level (there is a zero screw on most), but unless you are taking one from your boat to go flying, or plan to cruise in either the Dead Sea or Lake Titicaca you can safely assume that you are at sea level and the barometer reading needs no adjustment.

What matters is to be able to record changes of barometric pressure, rather than worry about the absolute accuracy of the reading.

Looking at my log of the 1979 Fastnet I see that the barometer read 990 mbs at midnight close SE of Cape Clear, then fell 10 mbs in 2½ hours as we were hit by the center of the notorious Low "Yankee" whose associated front did all the damage. Official meteorological jargon describes any fall of 6 mbs in three hours as "very rapid," so we were clearly heading for bad trouble, with the barometer falling twice as fast as the gloomiest language the Met Office permits itself. For the record, a "slow" rise or fall is less than 1 mb change in three hours; a "quick" one is 3.5 to 6 mbs in the same time, until it goes off the clock as above. At the time, the barometer's behavior had all the fascination of watching the needle of a submarine's depth gauge go down out of control.

Rather than make your on-board forecasts based on logged barometer readings, you can have them graphically displayed on a barograph plotting millibars against time. Mostly they have a clockwork-driven drum carrying a week's squared paper with a stylus tracing the pressure all the time. These are interesting but have drawbacks: no one is quite certain how much heavy weather motion they can stand up to, although makers claim they have them damped and resiliently mounted.

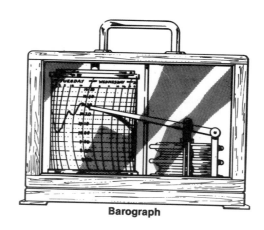

Barograph

Certainly they need to be securely installed well away from any other leads or sheets which might snag them. At around $400 they cost about five times as much as an analog barometer.

Weather forecasting

Some owners never miss a weather forecast while they are on board. By contrast Rod Stevens used not to allow a radio receiver on board for fear of the navigator or skipper taking the weather forecasts seriously and acting too soon by reducing sail on a storm warning, or too late in shaking out the reefs.

In the 1950s the Southsea-Brixham Race was won easily by *Prelude*. She was the only yacht in the fleet without a radio, so received no warning of a severe gale which never developed. All the others either put into Cherbourg or reefed down to a standstill.

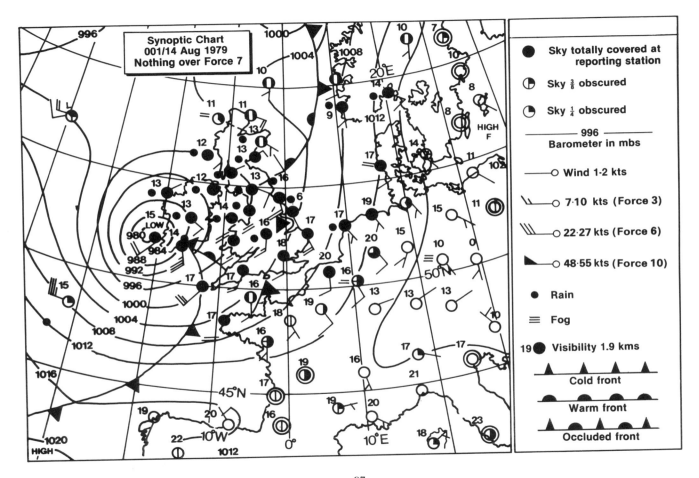

Synoptic Chart
001/14 Aug 1979
Nothing over Force 7

Sky totally covered at
reporting station

Sky ⅜ obscured

Sky ¼ obscured

———— 996 ————
Barometer in mbs

Wind 1·2 kts

7·10 kts (Force 3)

22·27 kts (Force 6)

48·55 kts (Force 10)

Rain

Fog

19 Visibility 1.9 kms

Cold front

Warm front

Occluded front

There are those who are uneasy if they have not nodded sagely over the synoptic chart, whether received on board by facsimile (weather fax), pinned up at the fuel pontoon in the marina or published alongside the crossword puzzle in the daily paper. Like all such graphic presentations they are no better than the met men ashore who have interpreted all the reports from weather ships, reporting stations and satellite observations. The end result is a synoptic chart showing the centers of Lows and Highs surrounded by isobars, which are contour-lines showing where the barometric pressure is the same (see p. 97). Since the wind flows towards areas of low pressure and away from the Highs it is necessary to understand two facts which follow this unsurprising doctrine:

(1) The greater the change in adjacent areas of barometric pressure the stronger the wind will blow to keep nature's weather systems in balance. So, close isobars mean strong winds. How strong can be reliably measured on a logarithmic scale usually printed on the synoptic chart.

(2) Due to the earth's rotation the winds do not flow directly towards the center of a Low at sea level. They also lose some of their power due to friction of the earth's surface. They form an anticlockwise pattern around the Low's center. Imagine it as a horde of Apaches racing in a circle around a beleaguered wagon train carelessly loosing off arrows inwards, but forgetting to allow for the 20 knots forward velocity of their horses—so their arrows don't go straight into the wagons, but obliquely at an angle of about 25° tangential to each contour or isobar. With a High system the winds blow outwards and clockwise to the area of high pressure, again about 25° away from the tangent.

As with the story about the swirl of the bathwater going down the drain, in the Southern Hemisphere it's all the other way round.

When interpreting a synoptic chart there are some simple notations which will help you assess the weather it is likely to presage.

Wind direction and strength are shown as arrows pointing the right way, with feathers sticking out of their weather ends. Each full feather denotes 2 points on the Beaufort Scale. Thus 3½ feathers would show Force 7.

In British waters, depressions (Lows) typically move ENE'ly through or to the north of the British Isles at speeds which can be as high as 70 knots, but mostly nearer the speed reported as "steadily" on shipping forecasts (15–25 kts). Sometimes they are held up by a persistent high pressure area and will slow down or even briefly stop. When they are dissipating they are referred to as "filling," but "deepening" is bad news—it means the pressure of the low is falling and, with it, the surrounding winds are sure to pipe up.

The master of the *Queen Elizabeth* once told me that he did not bother too much about depressions while on a crossing to the United States, because his ship was through and out the other side in a matter of a couple of hours, with 28 knots traversing an oncoming depression moving at the same speed, making the relative movement of the storm away from the liner nearly a mile a minute. But making a W-E crossing can be tedious. So it was in 1960 sailing *Drumbeat* from Newfoundland to Brixham, we picked up a slow-moving warm front soon after departure and stayed in its clammy claustrophobic grip most of the way across.

Different types of air masses in the vicinity of a Low jostle for position and form distinct boundaries or fronts with predictable weather behavior either side of them. Light warm air advancing in the south side of a Low runs with a cold mass, rises over it and creates heavy rain. The boundary is a warm front shown on weather charts as rounded nodules or bumps on its leading edge. The warm air behind it has little rain, but

Warm Front:
advancing warm air rides up and over cold air

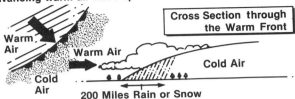

Cold Front:
advancing cold air pushes under the warm air

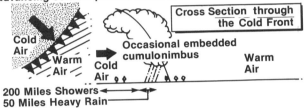

Occluded Front:
cold air has advanced on warm air and lifted it

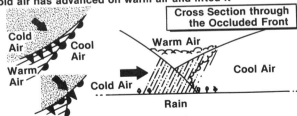

the wind direction veers markedly. Not far behind will be the cold front, bringing more rain, but clearing rapidly as it goes through and the wind veers still farther.

The cold front is shown as a line drawn out from the Low with spiky markings. When it overtakes and merges with the warm front, it is said to be occluded, shown by alternate spikes and nodules on the chart.

Hurricanes

During June to October tropical cyclones may form in mid-Atlantic in the doldrums and generally move in a sweeping clockwise path towards Florida, tracking north of the Caribbean to bounce off Cape Hatteras and sweep northeast with the Gulf Stream. Thereafter they lose their maximum ferocity of winds in excess of 100 knots in the open wastes of the North Atlantic. The still small eye of the storm can be as little as 2 miles across, but sometimes is up to 25 miles. Its speed of advance, which is accurately tracked and reported at least seventy-two hours ahead of time, is usually 10–15 knots, but can be considerably faster. The U.S. Weather Bureau puts out special bulletins at least four times a day reporting the position, course and speed of the center of each hurricane.

Hurricanes do not always conform to pattern. Some hurricanes go right on into the Gulf of Mexico and ravage Texas and Louisiana. Others have been known to strike inland through New Jersey to end their days in the mouth of the St. Lawrence River. Hurricane Charlie (feminists insisted that male names be added some years ago) made it all the way to the English Channel in 1986.

The best place for a yacht to be during a hurricane is secured and doubled up in a well-sheltered anchorage. If caught at sea, it's a matter of which survival tactics you believe in or suit your boat best. The prime rule is to head away from the eye of the storm by running at right angles to its track with the wind on or abaft the starboard beam. If the wind backs you, you are on the less dangerous side of the hurricane. If it remains steady you lie right in the path of the center. If it clocks or veers you are in trouble. Unless you react very early to the hurricane warnings and have faith in their prognosis, it is unlikely that you can move far enough in time to escape a hammering.

Sources of Weather Forecasts

The U.S. Weather Service broadcasts local weather reports continuously on VHF-FM 162.55 MHz (Channel 1). Alternate frequencies are 162.40, 163.75 or 169.075 MHz. Almanacs list the weather reporting channels for each locality along the coast from one of the following three:

WX1   162.55 MHz
WX2   162.4 MHz
WX3   162.75 MHz

Canadian weather reports are on Channel 21 (161.650 MHz) or Channel 83 (161.775 MHz). Storm warnings are broadcast on WWV (see p. 81).

In offshore waters weather forecasts may be broadcast on SSB by station WOO, WOM, WAH and WLO. (See almanacs or List of Radio Signals for times and frequencies.)

Around Britain the BBC's long wave 1500 m (200 kHz) forecasts are the most easily received. These are transmitted every day on clocktime at 0033, 0555, 1355 and 1850. There are inshore waters forecasts on Radio 3 247 m (12.15 kHz) at 0655 and on long wave at 0038. Besides the conventions already mentioned, the shipping forecasts use other definitions which it is as well to know:

A gale is said to be "imminent" if it is expected within six hours of the issuing time of the bulletin (usually one to two hours before transmission, but always stated).

If it is expected "soon" it is within six to twelve, while "later" means it is over twelve hours away.

In defining the visibility, it is "moderate" if 2–5 miles, "good" beyond that and "poor" down to $\frac{1}{2}$ mile when it is officially fog.

Storm cones are black triangular (or by night red lights) hoisted point downwards for gale-force winds due from or expected to move toward the south, which actually means anywhere from 091° through 180° to 269°. The cone point up covers gales from all other quarters of the compass.

Old salts' tales

There are many catch phrases which have survived since oilskins and seaboots were invented. They all have an odds-on chance of being right. For instance:

Red sky at night—sailor's delight
Red sky in the morning—sailor's warning

Then there are:

When the wind shifts against the sun,
Trust it not, for back it will run

When the wind follows the sun,
Fine weather will never be done

Long foretold—long past
Short notice—soon past

The cruel one, especially when it happens is:

First rise after very low
Indicates a stronger blow

We all know how an easterly wind pattern can persist:

If the wind be north-east three days without rain,
Eight days will pass before south again.

Clouds (see pp. 102–104)

It is almost self-evident that high, white, fluffy, soft clouds are friends telling you to expect fine weather with light to moderate breezes. Blacker and more ragged clouds presage hard weather.

High clouds moving in a different direction from lower ones indicate a change of wind direction.

A distant depression is often signaled by converging streaks of high cloud meeting at a point well over the western horizon; it may be 500 miles away at that time, but it could be with you in twelve hours.

From a clear blue sky to one in which day has been turned into night there is a wide variety of patterns aloft, any of which may contribute toward the navigator's understanding of what the weather is about to do. All glider pilots and most aviators brought up in unpressurized aircraft are good shipmates when it comes to recognizing turbulence and squalls under certain clouds. Some will go to extraordinary lengths to chase them when there's not much wind around elsewhere.

High Clouds (over 20,000 ft) indicate gentle conditions on deck, but some give early warning of changes to come.

Cirrus (Ci) are delicate white clouds which sometimes form those mares' tales with which old salts pepper their yarns. They tell you that there's a lot of wind up there, but nothing much will happen on deck in your watch.

Cirro-stratus (Cs) occurs when all the cirrus has spread into one transparent cloud covering most of the upper sky. Especially when accompanied by halos it indicates unsettled, deteriorating weather for sure.

Cirro-cumulus (Cc) are banks of small white clouds forming parallel bands across the sky, similar to patterns seen at low

tide on some sandy beaches. Changeable weather is on the menu, especially when it moves briskly.

Medium Clouds are those which determine one's comfort when flying in a light aircraft, being between 7,000 and 20,000 feet above sea level.

Alto-cumulus (Ac) are layers of gray or white clouds, similar to cirro-cumulus, but much lower. Sometimes known as a mackerel sky, it presages rain. If it forms patterns like the battlements of a castle, stand by for thunderstorms.

Alto-stratus (As) is an all-over lay of thin gray cloud through which a watery sun may appear. Rain is a certainty, probably with an approaching front bringing wind with it. When the rain comes, the cloud base may become very much lower, when it becomes Nimbo-stratus (Ns).

Low Clouds, below 7,000 feet, are the most familiar.

Cumulus (Cu) are the cottonwool clouds with gray bottoms. When they are not too large or reaching for the stars, they mean fair weather. But when they expand to look like giant cauliflowers, watch out for showers.

Cumulo-nimbus (Cb) are instantly recognizable as thunderclouds, high, flat-topped and unfriendly. They are to be found in the vicinity of active fronts, invariably with squalls and strong winds.

Stratus (St) are low, gray, miserable clouds, often sitting over headlands. They mean drizzle and poor visibility.

Strato-cumulus (Sc) are masses of gray puffy clouds, frequent in winter on those raw days of drizzle or sleet.

But the most welcome, and recognizable, sign in the sky is when the rain clouds end in a hard line across the western horizon, giving way to blue skies. That's the end of a front.

Local variations

The most common phenomena to upset the direction and speed of the winds all over the world are land and sea breezes.

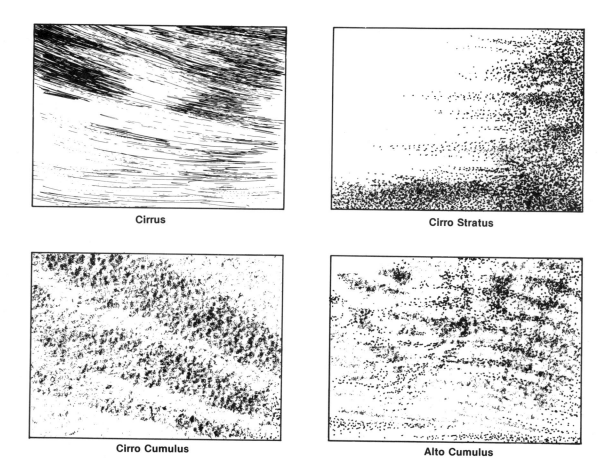

Cirrus

Cirro Stratus

Cirro Cumulus

Alto Cumulus

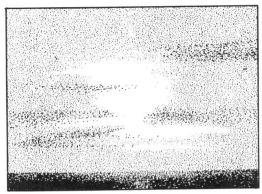

Alto Stratus

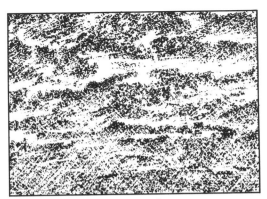

Strato Cumulus

Cumulus of the Doldrums

Cumulus

103

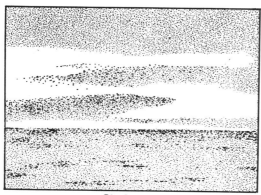

Stratus

Cumulo Nimbus

Line Squall

Not only are most winds much stronger away from land, excepting only those generated by a funneling effect in high-sided estuaries, but their direction and strength will change as the sun climbs into the sky. This is especially true when the underlying wind in the area is light. As the land warms up the sea breeze will fill in on an onshore direction, usually for about a mile, but sometimes as much as 10 miles. At night the reverse is true, with a local land breeze blowing offshore as the land cools off. This can play a vital part in racing, and it's worth recalling when cruising once the log speed drops below 2 knots.

The 1973 220-mile Seine Bay Race started off Southsea in near calm conditions. It ended thirty-six hours later with Sir Max Aitken's brand new 52-ft ketch *Perseverance* taking all the prizes by finishing over two hours ahead of the next boat.

"At last," the yachting correspondent of one of the nationals commented with unconscious irony, "Sir Max has got the boat he richly deserves."

"Rocketship," declared the designer modestly as he stepped ashore.

What actually happened was that our top Solent tactician, Bobby Lowein, opted to work across toward the Isle of Wight shore in anticipation of a land breeze developing out of Bembridge, since it had been a hot cloudless day. Alone of the fleet we slowly crabbed our way across the fairway into slack water off St. Helen's, the others all having to kedge in a foul tide near the Outer Spit buoy. Sure enough, an hour after dark a private reaching breeze sent us tramping on starboard tack, leaving the whole fleet for dead.

Unhappily it was the only major race she ever won, soon revealing most of the nasty habits ever built into a boat. To be competitive we needed to find 10 feet off her IOR rating. But she had her moment, thanks to our betting on the land breeze and ignoring the rhumb line.

The strength of land and sea breezes are in proportion to the contrast between day and night temperatures along the coast. There is one feature to be borne in mind: if there has already been a steady onshore wind all day as part of the local weather pattern, it may do no more than reduce its strength after nightfall, while the reverse will be found some hours after dawn if the sea breeze makes up in the same direction as the prevailing wind.

The global distribution of pressure and weather systems is well known, from the Doldrums of the equator, through the trade winds either side of them to the Horse Latitudes. Weather off the coasts of the United States is greatly influenced by local pressure systems, yet some generalization is possible. In the summer the prevailing winds from Florida to Newfoundland are sou'westerly. On the West Coast winds are mostly from the nor'west, under the twin influences of a High system over Hawaii and a Low to the east of the Rockies.

The British Isles lie in a belt modestly understated as Variable Westerlies, while the matching zone in the Southern Hemisphere is more aptly named as The Roaring Forties. All these have logical effects on ocean currents, the most famous of which is the Gulf Stream, funneled NNE'ly between Florida and the Bahamas. Its warm core sinuates in a broad clockwise sweep across the North Atlantic before splitting. One arm gives the farmers as far north as Tromsö, Norway, relatively easy winters and little ice in those northern fjords. It is also responsible for the Soviet Navy's having year-round access to the North Atlantic from the Kola Inlet. The other arm swings southwards past Galway and Kerry, sustains the tropical gardens at Tresco, sends early daffodil crops to Covent Garden, thence past the Iberian Peninsula before turning west near the Cape Verde Islands to pick up a fresh load of Sargassum weed and go round the track again.

The area of benign trade winds is also the breeding ground of savage hurricanes and cyclones with winds up to 170 knots, moving on (nowadays) well-reported tracks at speeds up to 300 miles per day during their appointed seasons. It is relatively simple and obviously prudent planning to avoid being exposed to these king-size storms.

Each year thousands of yachtsmen in small boats make the trade wind crossing from the Canaries to the Caribbean during our winter, outside the hurricane season. Most of them confidently look forward to successive days of brilliant sunshine, running wing-and-wing or tacking downwind across a cobalt sea with little to worry about beyond when to deep-six the bananas or whether the cold beer and suntan lotion will last the trip. Weather forecasts are not worth listening to.

In November 1979 I was two-thirds of the way to English

Harbor, Antigua, in the Swan 47 *Toscana* when a local storm hit us in the middle of the night. It behaved like a junior hurricane, gusted 50 knots and boxed the compass before leaving us within the hour to reset the sails, steady on 270° and get back into routine: identify the seabirds, pick up the dead flying fish (delicious, filleted and sautéed in butter), call the cook early and recalculate one's bet on the sweep for the noon-to-noon run. Research in the *Admiralty Sailing Directions* turned up an Inter Tropical Convergence Zone (ITCZ) storm, so local as often as to go unreported.

Such local freak storms can be found all over the world, many of them of lethal severity. The NW'ly mistral in the Gulf of Lions in winter and spring, the E'ly levanter bringing low cloud over the Rock of Gibraltar, the SE'ly sirocco and NE'ly gregale around Malta, the icy tramontana in the Tyrrhenian and Adriatic seas, like Santa Ana off the Southern California desert, williwaws off Patagonia, not to mention willy-willies off Queensland. Each has the power to hit like a heavyweight, landing the winning punch before the opponent has come out for the bell at the start of the round.

So it was at 1245 two days after Christmas 1977, in the Holland-designed Two-Tonner *Knockout*. We had reason to be pleased with our progress that far in trying to take the Sydney-Hobart trophy back to Britain. We had put 150 miles between us and the overkill of Sydney hospitality on a brilliant sunny day, 30 miles off the coast of New South Wales, with Mount Dromedary abaft the beam. Fixes showed that we had got the current we had come for. At 1110 the NW'ly breeze faltered, so we set the light blooper and ½ oz spinnaker, gossamer light but drawing like a poultice.

I was regaling the afterguard with how I first heard of fabric being like gossamer—in a mail-shot from a chemist in Piccadilly just after my engagement had appeared in *The Times*. Regular supplies of their product were offered in plain enve-

lopes. The sales-pitch ended with: "Finally, may we wish you every conceivable joy." At noon the weather forecast was for easterlies 25–30 knots off Gabo Island, 100 miles farther down the track, with a new front the next day bringing W or SW winds 20–30 knots, later going W or NW and moderating.

"That's an odd cloud across the horizon ahead," someone remarked. I had the *Australian Sailing Directions* in the cockpit, open at the picture of a typically white and inviting cloud formation heralding a Southerly Buster. A mile ahead a boat was seen to drop her spinnaker and harden in. Bobby Lowein, the best of many superb ocean-racing skippers I have been lucky enough to navigate for, called immediately for three reefs in the main and the tiny armor-plated No. 6 jib.

As the ripples came at us across the glassy sea, we just got the ½ oz down before being hit by a 40-knot southerly, right on the nose, building to a steady Force 10 in as many minutes.

The 1979 Fastnet should be in the *Guinness Book of Records* as the sporting event which claimed the greatest number of participants' lives—fifteen. Of the 302 boats which set out, 218 were officially deemed to have "retired," a euphemism which included five sunk and eighteen abandoned mostly with crippling damage. The forecasters' gale warnings, based on synoptic charts available to them, were too little and too late, nor were they sufficiently ominous. The official inquiry reached a few surprisingly complacent conclusions:

> In the Western Approaches to the British Isles gales which arrives with little warning are a feature of our weather which those who sail must expect to encounter from time to time.
>
> We can find insufficient evidence to lead us to recommend any alteration in the size limits for entrants.

Others did, noting that all the fatalities and all but one of the boats abandoned were in the three smallest classes—under 30 ft rafting at the time, or one-ton size and smaller. The lesson of the Sydney–Hobart Race only eighteen months previously had not been taken in. This time there were no handy ports of refuge to run for.

Here's how I saw it, as recorded in my deck log of the same *Toscana*, whose strong crew included John Rousmaniere, author of the best book about the disaster (*Fastnet-Force 10*). Soon after midnight on my birthday, August 13, we rounded Land's End and headed for the Fastnet Rock 150 miles away to the NW. A reaching SW breeze Force 4/5 died at breakfasttime, soon after the morning BBC Shipping Forecast, which spoke of SW Force 4–6. By noon the wind had backed to SSE 5–6, then veered to SW in 10 minutes, blowing out the ¾ oz chute.

At 1355 there was mention of a Low 300 miles to the west, but our area forecast remained SW 4–5, increasing 6–7 and going to the west. As we listened we were already sailing in a W x S wind Force 6, which then died to light southerlies.

At 1750 we got our first gale warning associated with low "Yankee," now said to be 250 miles west of the Fastnet. Our area (Lundy/Fastnet) was booked for S'ly Force 4, locally 6, increasing to gale Force 8 before going NW. At dusk the wind was still S'ly, but gusting over 40 knots, as we reeled off 9 knots along the rhumb line with a single-reefed main.

By midnight the barometer had fallen 10 mbs in 2½ hours to 980 mbs and we had a whole SSW'ly gale on our hands. Our sail plan now consisted of the smallest jib on the inner headstay, with all three reefs pulled down on the main. Sure enough, the 0015 shipping forecast told us what we already knew, except that Force 10 was mentioned for the first time. But we were comforted by the fact that the nearest reporting station (Valencia) only had S x E Force 6, although its barometer was 986 mbs and "falling rapidly."

The abrupt wind shift which did all the damage hit us about 10 miles ESE of the Rock. Five hours after rounding it the barometer had risen 12 mbs to 994 mbs.

Even if we had a radio weather-fax receiver we should have been none the wiser, for the official synoptic chart for midnight (see p. 97) did not carry any symbols for winds above Force 7, although the passage of the cold front which triggered off the cataclysmic wind veer is plain to see. When redrawn after the event, the wind velocities were remeasured from the isobars and nearly justified the velocities the fleet had to survive. Later weather guru Alan Watts produced an interesting theory that there had been undetected "ripples" along the isobars, which brought them very much closer to each other in places than the faired off lines on the synoptic chart indicated. Obviously, wherever that happened there would be gusts of great severity, which, he argued, would account for boats near each other reporting widely differing wind speeds.

I buy that. But the real lesson of both these big storms is that on-board observation of the behavior of the barometer and reading the cloud formations should have been enough to warn us. That's all very well if you're still in harbor or in coastal waters, but once offshore with nowhere to hide perhaps it's as well to imagine you are sailing with Rod Stevens and take the weather as it comes. No yacht can sail fast enough to clear the front of an advancing storm. Besides noting the behavior of your own barometer, be on the alert whenever land reporting stations report widely differing barometer readings on the same shipping forecast.

Ever since that Fastnet I suspect the lads at the Met Office have hedged their bets with such qualifying asides as: "Winds sou'west 4 to 5, perhaps locally 7 or 8 at times." That suffix would justify a gale warning being issued for the area, which played havoc with the jetfoil sailings on the Dover-Ostend route when they first started operating and were told not to sail if there was a gale warning in force. Some British listeners claim to recognize the duty forecaster by the degree of wariness built into his script.

I have not done a proper analysis, but I rely on forecasts' being right about 60 percent of the time. They claim 80 percent accuracy for land forecasts. The rest of the time they can lead people to hold onto a course far from the rhumb line in anticipation of a wind shift or encourage them to persist with the wrong sail plan long after it should have been changed.

Mostly, however, the forecasts tell you about the weather you've already got. And they do not have the data needed to give any warning about the seas likely to be encountered. So the combination of an angry sea from the WNW clashing with 20 ft swells from the SSW, which really killed most of the Fastnet fleet, could not possibly have been hinted at in any of the bulletins.

Currents

Of all the natural phenomena associated with the weather, the most predictable in their behavior, next to the times of sunrise and sunset, are the currents, whether wind-generated or tidal. The latter may be held up by persistent contrary winds and their heights vary in bottleneck harbors, but, as a rule, they come and go as stated in the tables and tidal atlases.

The direction of the various ocean currents may be relied on, although strengths may vary in proportion to surface winds' persisting for any length of time. The most famous of these is the Gulf Stream, especially as it affects yachts cruising or racing off the eastern seaboard of the United States with the violent local electric storms which prowl along its edges. The Newport-Bermuda Race is rarely won or lost without the stream's playing a part. It has a hot core of water about 10 miles wide carrying stream current water at its maximum of about 4 knots. Its presence is marked by a sudden jump in seawater temperature at its so-called west wall (the side facing the United States). This can be as much as 8–10° in a few hours, but the corresponding drop on the Bermuda side of the

core is not so marked and probably not more than 5° at the most.

The catch is that the core rarely flows steadily in a WSW-ENE'ly direction until it is well past Bermuda, but meanders as much as 70° off course for a distance of 30 miles or more, before swinging back to rejoin the grain of the stream. Sailing down from Newport, one's trick is to hit off the SE'ly meander and ride it for all it's worth, making 11–12 knots over the ground. If you guess wrong you will have to plug a foul current for many hours. Sometimes the stream water breaks away and forms circular eddies as much as 40 miles in diameter. Warm eddies rotate clockwise, so to hitch a ride on them you must hit one off nearly tangential to its eastern perimeter. Cold eddies are anticlockwise, so must be approached from their western side. This feature gave the race some unlikely winners and the soubriquet among the losers of being the "Gulf Stream crapshoot."

Recently the element of luck has been reduced by the Ocean Services Unit of the National Oceanic and Atmospheric Administration (NOAA) in Washington using its computers to produce tidal charts of the Stream based on data from satellite surveillance. The latitude-longitude of the points along the west wall and the centers of the identifiable eddies are broadcast on radio twice a day. With all that information on your plot, all you need do is navigate the boat to the point where it starts to be boosted along by favorable currents. Given Loran-C in good form, that is child's play.

As always, there are snags. The whole boiling issue moves in a generally ENE'ly direction at speeds which cannot be predicted with certainty. So if the satellite has an off day or has trouble delivering the raw data through total cloud cover, your plot may be two to three days out-of-date, thus leaving you guessing.

In the 1984 race there was a hefty SE'ly meander to be

found just west of the rhumb line. Most of the fleet hit it off, only to be greeted with 30–35 kt SE'ly winds over the deck all the way to the finishing line. That was a classic wind-against-tide situation, beating all the way down what is traditionally a brisk reaching course. It was a bit like opting to go through the Portland Race to get a fair tide. When the boat stopped slamming like a destroyer, it meant you'd left the strongest part of the current and it was time to tack back for more.

By contrast, the 1986 race laid on a barely discernible meander, but a huge cold eddy to the south of it. It was a reaching and running race of light airs. Armed with a private long-range met forecast of uncanny accuracy we caught all the wind shifts very early, hit off the western side of the cold eddy and finished fourth in the hottest IOR Class in an eight-year-old boat.

Although many cruising yachtsmen read about the Bermuda Race, their main interest lies in knowing where to put all the Gulf Stream data in perspective in planning a transatlantic passage. It may be summed up as follows:

(a) Its mean velocity is at its greatest between the Florida Keys and a point about 200 miles NNE of Bermuda, having swept close past the notorious Cape Hatteras. In that area will be found not only severe local storms and heavy seas, but always a strong current in a broadly NNE'ly direction, slowly turning eastwards.

(b) If on a west-to-east transatlantic passage it is always worth putting up with local discomfort for the bonus of its current. At least the seas in it are warm and there is a lot of sunshine between squalls. On an east-west crossing keep well clear, either using the Great Circle route far to the north, or the balmier trade wind crossing about 1,000 miles north of the equator. Many people make the mistake of an intermediate course from the Azores to the west. That usually means the worst of both worlds.

(c) If you have to cross the stream, treat it just like any other tidal current by laying off the amount you expect to be pushed laterally and adjusting course accordingly.

(d) Be on the conservative side with the sail area carried through the stream at night, unless you have a strong and alert crew.

Summary of on-board weather forecasting
Assuming a North Atlantic depression moving in a generally easterly direction, a tabulated checklist of the points to look for and what they mean is included here.

Humidity Professional forecasters set great store by observing changes in the atmosphere's relative humidity, but the instruments involved are not suitable for carrying in a yacht, so this aspect has been ignored.

Factor	Warm Front	Cold Front	Aftermath
Wind	Veers to SW and increases	Veers from SW to W or NW. Squalls, then decreases	Steady direction, moderating slowly
Barometer	Rapid fall ahead of the front	A sudden rise with the passage of the front	Gradually steadies
Air temperature	Warmer	Suddenly cooler	Steady
Visibility	Getting worse	Marked improvement behind the front	Much better
Sky and clouds	Clouding over from Cirrus to Nimbo-stratus	Strato-cumulus and Cu-nim in the front	Cumulus or blue sky
Rain	Steady, turning to drizzle on arrival of the front	Heavy rain	Occasional showers

110

First thoughts

Assuming you are not bent on qualifying for membership of the LYS (see back cover), the navigator has a formidable checklist to complete before setting sail for more than a day's picnic.

(1) *Destination*   Decide on sensible limits for your cruise, with the equivalent of diversionary airfields firmly identified. If any one in the crew has to be back in his office by a certain time, be sure there is no misunderstanding on that score. If he elects to come as far as Eleulthera with you, he'd better have his own plans for getting home, rather than rely on the boat to divert to Nassau for him. In any event, keep forty-eight hours in hand to allow for adverse weather on the return journey.

(2) *Speed of advance (SOA)*   While the carefree, one-day-at-a-time philosophy underlines the fact that you are cruising and not racing, it is as well to have a general understanding with the crew whether you are setting out on a voyage with a planned SOA of 4, 5½ or 7 knots. Some people think flopping around in crowded shipping lanes with a stalled anemometer is fun. Actually it is moderately dangerous, and the boat's motion can be tiresome. So have a clear policy about when the iron spinnaker is going to be pressed into service. Is it to be if the speed falls below 3 knots for, say, half an hour?

(3) *Route planning*   Do your preliminary planning on a small-scale chart covering the farthest extent of your cruise. For the English Channel Imray produce two excellent passage charts (C10 and 12) covering the whole area at 1:310,000 scale (4 nm to the inch). When you have a firm plan, buy the publications and large-scale charts you really need. At $12.25 each (and no doubt rising), you should shop carefully. The other day I drew

up a list of the absolute minimum inventory of charts and publications needed to get a friend's yacht from the Canaries to Dubrovnik, via the Balearics and Crete. The bill came to over $150.

(4) If you plan to go anywhere between the Bay of Biscay and West Germany, it is worth laying out £2.50 to get the Royal Yachting Association's publication *Going Foreign*, Volume I (CI / 87). It is available, along with other volumes covering different parts of the world, from the RYA, 22–24 Romsey Road, Eastleigh, Hants SO5 4YA (telephone: 0703-629962). Or you can consult the consulate of the country you are headed for.

Nearer the time

(1) Check that the crews all have passports with the necessary visas. Passports may never be called for, but local officials in newly independent nations tend to be inflexible and slow. Don't offend local dress conventions.

(2) Advise crews about stowage limitations and what to bring in gear, cash or kind to make it a harmonious cruise. It is not a bad idea to state a per diem mess bill to cover all the expenses you don't expect to meet yourself. Let them know whether they should bring their own bedding and / or safety harnesses. Say when duty free stores might be available. Have a note of their next-of-kin addresses and telephone numbers.

(3) Be sure the ship's papers are in order. If you don't have the official registration document between hardback covers, you must have irrefutable proof of ownership.

(4) Tell crews when to join and precisely where, giving your marina berth number where available.

(5) Take your national ensign, the flag(s) of countries to be visited for the starboard yardarm and a "Q" flag to be shown until cleared by customs and immigration (police) on arrival. In practice, even at large ports of entry like Cherbourg, you may have difficulty in finding anyone to pay the slightest attention to your arrival. However, you can count on the man collecting harbor dues to show up, and possibly the agent for duty-free stores.

(6) Check over all nav-aids, including the charts and electronics, especially the navigation lights. Have the ship's batteries at the top of a charge. Secrete your own private flashlight, pencil, matches and small batteries.

(7) Have firearms under lock and key.

(8) Make sure medical stores are up to inventory and in-date.

Last things

(1) Get a weather forecast from any source you think worth contacting. If cruising in British waters, try the new Marinecall service on 0898–500 450 for a marine forecast up to five days ahead.

(2) Decide upon and announce the time of sailing, so that you don't have to go ashore and press-gang the other watch.

(3) Clear customs, no matter how irksome or difficult that may be.

(4) Make sure the right sails are bent on. Decide what to do about the dinghy.

(5) Land all disposable waste.

(6) Top up consumables as required: water, fuel, ice.

(7) Check over emergency drills with the crew: man overboard, fire and collision. Here it might be worth a gentle reminder about the Rule of the Road (International Regulations for Preventing Collisions at Sea), since few yachtsmen know them as well as they should. What lights are shown by a tug with a long tow over 200 meters? Answer: three white vertical lights in place of her masthead light. What fog signal should a sailing yacht make? Answer: one long and two short blasts at intervals of not less than two minutes.

(8) Show where the following are stowed:
Safety harnesses, lifejackets and the life raft
Flashlights
Flares
Radar reflector
Foghorn and spare aerosol.

(9) Set the watches. Announce mealtimes and rules about drinking (if any).

GLOSSARY

analog: clock-face display.

anemometer: instrument showing relative wind speed.

antenna: aerial.

azimuth: true bearing in degrees.

barograph: barometer recording pressure readings on squared paper marked off in hours and days, usually for seven days.

Beaufort scale: table of wind forces, speeds and consequential effects.

beta light: fluorescent lighting for instruments, using tritium gas capsule.

BFO: beat frequency oscillator for cutting out background noise in receiving Morse, notably on radio D/F receivers.

Bracknell: headquarters of the British weather forecasting service.

chart scales: ratio from which miles per inch of each chart can be deduced. Usually expressed as 1:50,000 (say).

clew: the corner of a sail to which its sheets are made fast.

clinometer: an instrument showing the angle of heel either side of vertical.

cold front: a line of weather associated with a center of low barometric pressure, bringing its own characteristic weather behavior. It usually follows a warm front.

compass rose: 0°–360° graduations arranged as a circle on a chart, aligned to True North, usually on a meridian of longitude. A concentric arrow shows the direction of magnetic north, the Variation and rate of change each year.

contour: a line on a chart indicating the steps in the heights or depths. The 3-meter or 2-fathom line is a contour.

"cut": the expression used by British navigators to give the precise moment of taking an altitude, range or bearing. Equivalent to U.S. "mark."

datum: the baseline for any hydrographic measurements of height or depth.

DC: direct current, as opposed to AC, which is alternating current.

Decca: British hyperbolic aid giving continuous fixes within its coverage.

declination (dec): the altitude of a heavenly body N or S of the equator at any given moment.

deckwatch: a chronometer with its error recorded daily, formerly kept for timing celestial observations.

depth-sounder: a device for measuring the depth by electronic impulses. Also known as an echo sounder or fathometer (U.S.).

D/F: direction finding, usually by measuring known sources of radio signals.

deviation: the error of the ship's magnetic compass on any heading, measured in degrees and fractions W or E of the accurate magnetic heading.

digital: instrument readings shown as numerals constantly varying to display navigational data (e.g., courses, speeds).

dividers: an instrument for taking distance measurements off a chart by a tipped pointer on each of its two legs.

doppler: the effect of sound or radio waves changing their pitch as they approach and then leave the listener.

DR: dead reckoning, a position arrived at by using only the logged distance, without applying tidal current, leeway or windage.

DWE: the deckwatch error recorded in minutes and seconds against a time-signal.

effective temperature: a measurement of the temperature you feel, as opposed to that which the thermometer shows. It takes into account wind speed and is known in the United States as "wind-chill factor."

EP: Estimated Position. The DR corrected for all other known or assumed factors affecting the ship's position.

equinox: the date around March 23 and September 23 when the sun is precisely over the equator at noon and there are equal hours of day and night. Associated with equinoctial gales.

eyes (of the boat): the foremost point of the upper deck.

fax: a document transmitted by radio and received as a precise copy; i.e., facsimile. A weather fax gives the receiving boat a synoptic weather chart as a direct printout.

fix: a position on a chart showing the boat's position at any time with complete certainty.

fluxgate compass: the device at the heart of most automatic steering systems. It is not north-seeking, but will continue to point in any given direction until told to do otherwise.

–g: deceleration at units of 32 ft per second^2.

GHA: the Greenwich Hour Angle of a heavenly body measured 0°–360° westward from the Greenwich meridian around the equator.

gimbals: a mounting for keeping anything in the horizontal or vertical plane regardless of the heel of the ship (compasses, lamps, stoves, etc.).

GMT: the time kept between 7½°W and 7½°E without local adjustments such as Summer Time. It is the base for all tables and calculations in celestial navigation.

113

gnomonic: a chart drawn so that all the meridians of longitude meet at either pole, as on any globe.

GP: the geographical position of any heavenly body, which is the point on the earth's surface directly underneath it. It is a function of declination and hour angle.

GPS: Global Position System, a means of giving continuous fixes of high accuracy anywhere in the world. Not yet available to yachtsmen.

Great Circle: the shortest track between any two points on the earth's surface drawn as a straight line on a gnomonic chart, or as a curved one on a Mercator chart, except for courses due N or S.

Greenwich meridian: the N-S line from which all longitude scales are graduated E or W. It happens to pass through the Astronomer Royal's old telescope just up the hill from the National Maritime Museum at Greenwich.

H$_C$: the tabulated or calculated altitude of any heavenly body at the time of a simultaneous direct observation.

H$_O$: the corrected observed altitude taken at the same time as H$_C$.

HE: the height-of-eye above the water when taking any observation. Its correction was formerly known as Dip.

hockey puck: U.S. slang for a small rubber-framed hand-bearing compass.

hotel load: the electrical power needed to sustain the basic requirements of any boat with electrical instruments and appliances—all the way from navigation lights to freezers.

horizontal parallax: an allowance made for the moon because of its relative closeness to offset the fact that its rays do not hit the earth's surface at a single point, but in parallel bands.

hull speed: the theoretical maximum speed of a boat under sail before it planes. It relates to waterline length.

hygrometer: an instrument for reading the specific gravity of the electrolyte in a wet battery. The most accurate measurement of a battery's state of charge.

hyperbolic aids: navigation aids dependent on radio waves emanating from known shore stations, not dissimilar to the ripples on a pool after a stone has been thrown into it. Decca and Loran-C are examples.

IALA: the International Association of Lighthouse Authorities who seek universal adoption of uniform buoyage and light systems.

impeller: the moving part in a log measuring speed (and distance) by the rotation of a small helical vane let into a protective skeg.

IMS: the International Measurement System, which assesses racing handicaps for boats predominantly intended for cruising.

Inertial Navigation: a means of fixing position by very accurate small gyros and their associated accelerometers measuring the variance from N and S coordinates. Not yet available for yachts.

index error: the error in measuring sextant altitudes due to the zero point on the scale being out of alignment.

intercept: the measured distance which a single position line of a celestial body is from the position arbitrarily assumed for calculating a sight.

IOR: the International Offshore Rule for handicapping yachts. Over the years it has favored boats with speed but few other attributes.

isobars: lines of equal barometric pressure on a weather map.

isophase: a navigational light which shows its light and eclipse periods at exactly similar intervals.

Jeppesen plotter PJ 1: a light aircraft protractor which is the best for plotting in yachts as well. U.K. equivalent is Airtour navigation plotter (ANZP-1).

kHz: kiloHertz, the measurement of radio frequencies. Formerly known as kilocycles (kc/s).

land breeze: a breeze found in inshore waters after sunset on a long hot day, blowing away from the beach.

LAT: Lowest Astronomical Tide. As the name implies it is the lowest level of water ever to be expected at a given point. For practical purposes it differs little from Low Water Springs.

latitude: lines parallel to the equator marking degrees of arc as projected from the center of the earth from 0°–90°N or S at the poles. Each degree is 60nm, subdivided by 60 seconds of arc, each of one nautical mile. It is the standard scale for all measurements of distances at sea.

lead line: a traditional line with 3 kg lead for hand sounding.

leeway: the amount a yacht makes sideways due to the inadequacy of its keel or underwater profile.

LHA: local hour angle, measured E or W in degrees and seconds of arc from the observer's meridian.

LL: the lower limb (edge or rim) of the sun or the moon.

longitude: the E-W scale marked off on parallels of latitude. On a Mercator chart each degree decreases in size as the latitude approaches the poles. Also marked off in 60 seconds of arc for each degree.

Loran-C: the U.S. hyperbolic aid to yacht navigation corresponding to Decca with longer range and different coverage, but comparable accuracy.

lubber's line: the fore-and-aft line in the steering-compass assembly from which the course can be read off.

ma: milliampere, a measurement of very small amounts of electrical current.

"mark": the U.S. equivalent of "cut."

maxi: a racing yacht of or near 83 ft LOA. The generic term for all but the very biggest yachts of over 35 m length (megayachts).

mbs: millibars, the unit of barometric measurement.

meander: how the hot, fast core of the Gulf Stream strays off its grain before rejoining it.

Mer-Alt: the meridian-altitude of any heavenly body at its highest.

Mercator: the ancient navigator who introduced charts with all the longitude lines running N and S at right angles to the parallels of latitude.

meridian: a line of longitude.

Mer-Pass: the time of meridian-altitude.

monocular: an optical instrument with a single eyepiece.

Nautical Almanac: a publication giving all the ephemeral data (those which constantly change) for celestial navigation, times of rising and setting. Identical publications under the same name on both sides of the Atlantic.

Navtex: a printout of weather and navigation messages transmitted by radio and received on board like a telex.

Neaps: the tides having the lowest range, or difference between HW and LW.

NOAA: the National Oceanographic and Atmospheric Administration in Washington, D.C., which monitors weather, tides, ocean currents and the environment at sea.

Notices to Mariners (N to Ms): weekly publications put out by the Hydrographer of the Navy carrying all corrections to Admiralty charts and publications.

null: the lowest audible point, sometimes silent altogether, when swinging across a radio bearing for D/F readings.

observed position (Obs Pos): fix using celestial observations only.

parallel ruler: rulers for chartwork which can transfer a course or line of bearing laterally from one part of the chart to another.

pelorus: a stand on which the steering compass is mounted.

period: (1) the interval in the seconds between the passing of two successive wave-tops. (2) the time taken for a rhythmic light to complete one complete sequence of its stated characteristics; e.g., Fl$(_3)$W10s means a period of 10 seconds during which there are 3 flashes followed by an eclipse, all adding up to 10 seconds.

perpendicularity: the error in a sextant when the index mirror does not lie in the same plane as the arc showing degrees and minutes of altitude.

polar boat speed: a diagram constructed from theoretical data showing a boat's potential speed at various points of sailing in different winds.

position line: the endless line drawn at right angles to the azimuth of a celestial body used in laying off the distance equivalent to the intercept. The observer's position lies somewhere on that line.

PPI: plan position indicator. Radar display on cathode ray tube usually with own position in its center.

protractor: an instrument used for laying off or measuring angles, courses or bearings on a chart.

quadrantal error: the error in radio D/F induced by the materials or method of construction of any yacht.

Racon: a radar beacon on shore which paints its bearing on the PPI of the transmitting yacht's radar. Its effective range is 10 miles.

radar: a transmitted radio impulse which measures range and bearing of any object within its range and usually paints them onto a cathode ray tube, often referred to as a PPI (plan position indicator).

radar interceptor: a receiver intended to warn one that another radar is sweeping over you.

radar reflector: a metallic device which reflects radar waves from another source and gives an enhanced echo.

reciprocal bearing: a bearing 180° away from true.

reduction tables: special tables for working out astro-nav sights embodying all the permanent data, such as calculated altitudes, azimuths and declinations.

relative bearing: a bearing measured from the fore-and-aft line of the boat. Some use a 0°–360° clockwise scale starting from the stem-head. The Royal Navy use Red 0°–180° and Green 0°–180°. Thus relative 270° is the same as Red 90°.

relative wind: the direction of the wind felt over the boat. Often referred to as apparent wind. It applies to relative wind speeds.

RG: the symbol for a shore-based, radio-direction-finding station which will give a yacht the bearing of its transmission from it.

rhumb line: a course drawn as a straight line on a Mercator chart.

RORC: the Royal Ocean Racing Club, administrator of offshore racing in the U.K.

running fix: a fix derived from two bearings of (usually) the same object with the first one transferred after a substantial bearing change to give a fix. Its accuracy depends on knowing the course and speed between successive bearings accurately.

RYA: the Royal Yachting Association, the national authority for all forms of pleasure sailing and powerboat activities in the U.K.

SAR: Search and Rescue organization.

Sat-Nav: an instant fixing aid based on transmissions received from satellites passing overhead.

sea breeze: a wind which makes up from the sea during the forenoon of a hot day. It usually dies before dusk.

sea state: a scale of wave heights used in the United States, but not Britain.

semidiameter: the radius of the sun or the moon, always listed in almanacs.

sensors: any instrument used to detect or collect extraneous data. Thus a wind-direction and speed masthead fitting is a sensor.

side error: the error on the sextant when the horizon and index glasses are not in the same plane, so that the observed and reflected images of the sun do not coincide.

skeg: a fin attached to the bottom of the hull to carry the rudder. Can describe the keel itself when it is deep and narrow.

SOA: speed of advance (along the rhumb line).

SOG: speed over the ground on the course being made good.

sonic log: a means of measuring speed through the water by using two transducers to measure signals alternately transmitted with and against the water-flow.

tack: corner of the leading edge of a sail secured down before hoisting.

taffrail: the guardrail across the transom or stern of the boat.

transducer: inboard hull-fitting for echo sounder. Can send and receive.

transit: two prominent shore objects brought into line.

Transit: the U.S. satellite system which feeds Sat-Nav.

transponder: a radar reflector which receives a radar signal and sends it back greatly amplified.

UL: the upper limb (edge or rim) of the sun or moon.

variation: the angle to be applied to correct magnetic to true bearings or courses.

vertical sextant angle: the altitude obtained of an object of known height for determining its distance away.

VHF R/T: radio-telephony using Very High Frequency.

Vmg (velocity made good): speed through the water in the direction of true wind.

warm front: a line of weather associated with a center of low barometric pressure, with its own characteristic weather behavior. It usually precedes a cold front.

waypoint: positions preset into a Decca or Loran-C receiver as points where alterations of course are planned.

windage: the amount by which a boat is set sideways off its course by the action of the wind on its hull and superstructure.

wind sheer: U.S. description of the difference between the wind strength and direction on the water against that near the masthead.

zenith: the point in the sky directly overhead from the observer.

zone (time): bands of longitude each 15° across which keep the same clock time. Clocks are arbitrarily adjusted in units of one hour, so that all parts of the globe on the same latitude have sunrise and sunset at about the same clock time.

ZD: zenith distance is the angular difference between the zenith and the body observed. It is 90° minus the observed altitude.